10-MINUTE

CRYSTAL HEALING

Inspiring | Educating | Creating | Entertaining

Brimming with creative inspiration, how-to projects, and useful information to enrich your everyday life, quarto.com is a favorite destination for those pursuing their interests and passions.

10-MINUTE

CRYSTAL HEALING

Easy Tips for Using Crystals for
Healing, Shielding, and Protection

WRITTEN BY

ANN CRANE

FAIR WINDS

Contents

Introduction

Crystals have been used since ancient times by cultures all around the world to heal, protect, empower, divine the future, and so much more. These natural wonders, formed over millions of years, are an astonishing source of energy that anyone can harness to improve themselves and their life. This book will show you how.

You may already have a selection of beautiful crystals on your window ledge or wear certain stones as jewelry. Whatever your initial contact, crystals are here to help you connect to and amplify your own powers of manifestation. Not only are they the treasures of the Earth, they are as much a part of the universe as you are, so treat them with respect. They have ancient heritage and amazing powers.

All crystals and gemstones vibrate to what is known as the piezoelectric effect, discovered by French physicist and chemist Pierre Curie (1859–1906). What happens, in a technical sense, is that when mechanical stress is applied to the crystal, a voltage is produced across the crystal's surface. In fact, when you hold a crystal tightly in your hand and "warm it up," you are doing exactly that—applying stress so that its electromagnetic force comes alive. This effect is reversible, and if the polarity of the voltage is alternated, the crystal will rapidly expand and contract, producing a vibration. This is the key to the way quartz watches work.

So, an "alive" yet dormant crystal carries powerful Earth energy. Yet like everything in the universe it is also infused with the divine force that permeates all. This electromagnetic energy, or invisible force, is the bridge between its resonance both to you and the universe. Of course, crystals can be used merely for decorative purposes and personal adornment, but they are also important for enhancing you and your environment.

While the possibilities of what you can do with crystals are endless, this book focuses on their healing properties. Whether you want to bring your chakras back into alignment, mend a relationship, restore your spiritual balance, or protect your mind and spirit from outside forces, you will find something here for you.

How to Use This Book

Part One will introduce you to the world of crystals. You'll discover what crystals are, how they work, and some of the most common ways to use them. There are some great tips for those who are new to working with healing stones, including how to select, cleanse, and dedicate your crystals prior to working with them. You'll learn some simple ways to begin sensing crystal energy on your own so that you can tune in and "feel" what your stones can do for you. This section also covers the significance of different shapes and colors of crystals and provides information on the corresponding chakras and zodiac signs.

Part Two is a guide to simple ways you can use individual crystals for various kinds of healing: chakra healing, emotional healing, spiritual healing, and shielding or protection. These chapters will help you easily find what you're looking for, but since crystals are dynamic and multifaceted, you will find that their properties often fit into more than one category. A great way to get to know the stones in this guide is to read about one or two of your favorite crystals, followed by one that may be new to you. In this way, you're not only deepening your connection to your old favorites, but you'll also create some exciting connections with new healing stones.

Let your crystal journey begin.

PART ONE

CRYSTAL HEALING BASICS

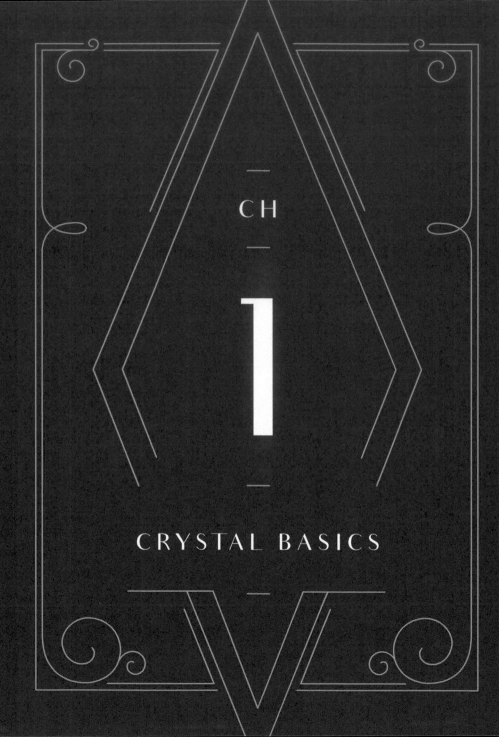

CH

1

CRYSTAL BASICS

C rystal healing has been used for thousands of years to shift the energy of mind, body, and spirit. Based on principles of both physics and metaphysics, crystal healing promotes positive change in the human energy field.

A crystal is a mineral with a regularly repeating molecular structure. Most crystals form inside the Earth during a process called nucleation, in which intense heat and pressure cause their molecules to form a three-dimensional lattice structure—like a blueprint. This geometric arrangement forces the crystal's molecules to take on the most stable form possible by repeating this pattern until the crystal is fully formed.

But crystals are more than just matter and molecules. The perfect, stable structure of a crystal represents the balance and harmony that most people seek in their own lives. As gifts from the Earth, healing crystals are symbols of balance and perfection from which you can begin your own transformation into the whole, healthy, balanced being you're meant to be.

Having crystals in your energy field balances your body, mind, and spirit.

CRYSTAL PROPERTIES

Because of their internal crystalline lattice, crystals are able to absorb and transmit light. This property, called refraction, allows crystals to draw in universal light energy, to reflect and refract it within their structure, and then transmit it back into the universe. The light energy is amplified and enhanced by the crystal's internal structure. All crystals are natural amplifiers of energy and assist personal healing by magnifying both the universal light energy that surrounds them as well as your intention for using them, and it is this that makes them such powerful healing tools.

Each crystal has its own unique vibrational frequency, just as each person has their own energy vibration; the interaction you have with a specific crystal will be unique to you. You may find that you connect deeply with some crystals but not with others. Because of the subjective nature of crystal healing, it is best to use stones to facilitate energetic shifts, which can create an overall sense of wellness, rather than a symptom-based approach.

THE HISTORY OF CRYSTAL HEALING

Crystals have been revered for thousands of years for their healing, divination, and other qualities by people from all over the globe including Chinese, Native American, Hebrew, Egyptian, Mayan, Greek, and Aztec societies. These sacred stones were first used as items of adornment, but the human relationship with the mineral kingdom soon evolved and ancient peoples began to recognize the energetic qualities of crystals. It is thought that as long ago as 25,000 BCE, specific stones were used for health, love, luck, and spirituality. There is documented use of the healing properties of crystals dating from 1500 BCE in the Egyptian medical text, the Ebers Papyrus.

Although not yet fully accepted by modern Western medicine, the use of crystals as a healing tool has been growing in popularity for decades. There are now many people searching for modern holistic healing methods who feel drawn to using crystal energy to bring balance to body, mind, and spirit.

WAYS TO USE HEALING CRYSTALS

Nothing much has changed since humans first began using crystals thousands of years ago, except these days we have access to a larger choice of stones than ever and many more people around the world are becoming aware of the power of crystals. So, let's have a look at what you can use your beautiful stones for.

Maybe you read about the properties of a stone and felt called to have it in your life. You rushed out and purchased it only to have it sit around and collect dust because you're not sure how to use it. So what can you actually do with your healing crystal? Well, crystals and stones can be used for many different purposes—including healing, divination, meditation, energetic cleansing, intuitive development and astral travel, and personal growth.

As you begin to dive in and use your crystals, it's highly recommended that you keep a journal of your experiences. For each new way that you use your stones, as well as for each new crystal, you should add an entry to your journal describing the stone you used, how you used it, and what your results were. This journal will help you not only to track your progress as you develop your healing skills, but it also acts as an excellent tool for discovering exactly how your crystals work best for you. Make time every few months to look back through the pages of your journal; you may begin to see patterns emerging in your entries. This journal is not only a tool for learning about your stones, but is also a powerful medium for self-discovery.

CRYSTALS FOR HEALING

Crystals are powerful healing tools. Healing stones balance and align the chakras and the aura. Crystal energy works on a subtle level, transforming the energetic roots of disease in the body. For this reason, crystals are a wonderful complement to traditional medicine. However, they should never be used to replace conventional treatments. While traditional medicine uses a symptom-based approach to healing, crystals are more integrative, creating energetic shifts that support physical and emotional healing.

Crystal healing is holistic and can be used to realign our energy so that we are healed emotionally, spiritually, and physically. For spiritual healing, where we need to reconnect to our soul or the universe, or simply gain a renewed sense of our spiritual self, we can meditate with certain crystals, such as amethyst, celestite, or moonstone. But for emotional healing, you can use a range of crystals to boost your well-being, balance your chakra energies, and enhance your emotions and general psychological state. For instance, red garnet balances sexual energy levels and alleviates emotional disharmony, while brown jasper stimulates the immune system. You will learn more about which crystals can be used for which purposes in Part Two.

Divination: Crystal divination is the art of using crystals to help you tap into your innate psychic gifts in order to receive guidance on your life path. Crystal divination can take many forms, including scrying, crystallomancy, and lithomancy. Crystal scrying utilizes slabs of stone like obsidian for gazing in order to view images and symbols that represent important concepts and themes in your life. Crystallomancy is the art of scrying with a crystal ball, typically made of clear quartz, which is used in a similar way to the obsidian mirror. Lithomancy, or stone casting, is an ancient practice of divining with stones. Stones are cast into a designated area, then read according to their properties, their relationship to one another within the casting area, and whether or not they fall within the casting area. Quartz crystal spheres have long been used for crystallomancy, a form of scrying divination.

Like many forms of magic and divination, crystals correspond to symbolic languages such as astrology, tarot, runes, and feng shui. Because crystals' vibrational power connects them to the universe, they can be used as a conduit or channel for cosmic knowledge from the past, present, and future.

Meditation: Meditating with crystals is a powerful way to connect with their energy. They can be quick and easy or deeply intense sessions— create a meditation routine to suit your own needs. Hold your crystal while meditating to tune into its energy and create a personal connection.

Cleansing: Crystals can also be used for energetic cleansing. They can be used to remove negative energy, self-limiting beliefs, and worn-out belief patterns and thought forms. Your stones are highly protective when worn or carried with you.

Intuition: Connecting with the energy of your stones during meditation or through divination is an easy way to develop your intuitive guidance. Some crystals can help you open up to universal source energy and connect with your spirit guides, angels, and animal spirits when placed in your sacred space. Stones can also be used for astral travel, dream healing, and more. Simply place the crystals in your pillowcase or on your bedside table.

Personal Growth: One of the most amazing ways to utilize your crystals is for your own personal growth and development. Any of the techniques mentioned on the previous page will strengthen your connection to crystal energy and move you toward spiritual ascension. Healers and shamans have used crystals for centuries to enhance intuition and facilitate mystical experiences.

Protection: Due to the electromagnetic energy exuded and absorbed by crystals, many can be used to protect you from the negative psychic energy of others or simply from geopathic stress around you. The Earth has a natural energy field and geopathic stress occurs when something disturbs this flow of energy, either above or beneath the Earth's surface. This can be anything from a diverted water course under your house, electric pylons near your home, or blocked ley lines, to springs and electric cables beneath your feet, underground trains, and fissures in nearby rocks. Crystals such as black tourmaline, obsidian, and smoky quartz can be placed in the home to absorb negative energy.

You can also wear or carry crystals to protect you from the negative energy of others. For example, you may have envious colleagues or neighbors, a difficult partner, or experience discomfort in a crowd. Wearing amber will protect you from the toxic or polluted thoughts of others, while carrying fluorite will guard you from general geopathic stress in the environment.

CRYSTAL SHAPES

There is a great deal of controversy in the crystal-healing community about which crystal shapes are best to use for healing. Some healers prefer natural rough stones because they feel the energy is stronger or more pure. These crystals—massive chunks of stone, geodes or clusters, or crystal points—have not been shaped or changed in any way. Other healers prefer to use shaped stones like tumbled or polished crystals or carved shapes. No matter which you prefer, it's helpful to have a variety of crystal shapes available in your collection so that you can gain experience in working with different types of energy.

Tumbled/polished: These are rough crystals that have undergone a process where they are put into a rotating cylinder with a series of abrasives until the rough edges become smooth and rounded. Tumbled stones are typically inexpensive compared to mineral specimens like points and clusters. They are great for using in a medicine pouch, or to travel with, as they are sturdy and have no breakable points. The energy of tumbled stones is very gentle and is much less intense than that of crystal clusters or points. For this reason, these stones are great for people who are highly sensitive to crystal energy. Unlike a crystal point, which has a very direct and focused energy, the energy in a tumbled stone radiates evenly from the center of the stone outward. Water-worn crystals are a form of naturally tumbled stones, but they are dull instead of showing the glossy surface exhibited by tumbled crystals.

Slabs/plates: This shape is a thin slice of stone. They can be used for cleansing and charging other crystals by placing the stones on top of the slab.

Rough: These stones have rough, often jagged surfaces, and look just as they did when they were taken from the Earth. Rough stones may be found as massive chunks, or they may have points or clusters of crystals. Most healers agree that the energy of these stones is very strong, so much so that it can feel too intense to people who are sensitive to energy. However, this intense energy can also be beneficial for diffusing energy and breaking up stagnant areas in the aura. This powerful vibration is very direct and works to create a rapid shift in the energy field of the user.

Carved totems: Crystal carvings can be shaped into a wide variety of figures or symbols, which commonly include animals, deities, hearts, stars, and others. Crystals carved into the shape of a deity are especially sacred because they embody the spirit and energy of that deity. When a crystal is carved into these shapes, they take on the properties and attributes of that figure in addition to the healing properties of the stone. For this reason, you can choose a stone that enhances the attributes of the figure or one that balances the qualities. For example, if you were choosing a carving of a heart, a stone like rose quartz would enhance the symbolism of love associated with the heart symbol. On the other hand, a stone like black tourmaline, which is more known for shielding and protection, would balance the attributes of compassion associated with the heart.

Palm stones and cabochons: Cabochons are commonly used in jewelry and have a flat back with a slightly domed surface. Palm stones are similar in shape, but both of the main surfaces are domed so that the overall shape looks similar to a bar of soap. These shapes are associated with protection, as they look similar to a shield. These crystals are also connected to vitality and prosperity.

Crystal balls: Crystal balls are perfect spheres carved from stone. This shape is known for enhancing intuition and psychic skills. The energy of a crystal ball is connected with wholeness and completion; it is a metaphor for the infinite. Spheres, like tumbled stones, emit gentle energy equally in all directions. They have been used for crystallomancy throughout history. One of the most famous crystallomancers was John Dee, adviser to Queen Elizabeth I. They are also a favorite of massage therapists, who occasionally use them as tools to massage the large muscles of the body.

Seer stones: Also known as riverbed quartz, these are specially shaped stones, typically made from quartz-based minerals, that are used for scrying divination. To create the seer stone shape, rough crystals are lightly tumbled to give them a round shape and wear away any jagged edges. Then, the stones are sandblasted, which creates a cloudy appearance similar to etched glass. Finally, the stones are cut in half and the cut edge is highly polished, creating a window-like surface. This clear face can be gazed at and the viewer can look into the depths of the crystal. Unlike a crystal ball, which is often completely transparent and easy to see through, the sandblasted surface of the seer stones creates a backdrop for the inner landscape of the crystal. These stones are typically inexpensive and make excellent scrying tools for beginner diviners. In a similar way to crystal balls, seer stones can be useful for enhancing intuition and psychic skills.

Eggs: Egg-shaped crystals have a natural affinity to the concepts of fertility, creativity, and new beginnings. This shape is commonly used as a tool for assisting healers when scanning the aura in order to detect energy imbalances. Eggs can be used for acupressure by gently pressing the more slender end into trigger points on the body. They can also be used for crystal massage.

Pyramids: Pyramid-shaped crystals have a flat square base and four triangular sides that join at an apex. This shape has a history going back thousands of years, associated with amplification of energy and intention as well as preservation. They are perfect for enhancing meditation and all spiritual growth work. Additionally, pyramids can be used to send distance healing to others and to project energy to other locations. They are also associated with prosperity and cleansing.

Vogel-cut crystals: These crystals are named after Dr. Marcel Vogel, a scientist and proponent of crystal energy healing. Dr. Vogel did lots of experimentation with crystal energy and determined that the energy of a crystal was strongest and most intensely focused when it was faceted into a wand with sides in multiples of twelve (12, 24, etc.). These wands are typically made of varieties of quartz crystal—clear quartz, amethyst, smoky quartz, rose quartz, citrine, etc.—and have terminations on either end. Vogel triangles are double-sided, with four smaller, faceted triangles on each side (pointing in opposite directions), which means that when looking through the triangle, you can see a Star of David shape. These are very powerful shapes and are typically reserved for very intense healing work, such as psychic surgery.

Massage and reflexology wands: These stones have been cut and polished into a long, slender, wand-like shape. Massage wands are rounded on both ends, typically with one narrow end to be used for small areas like the face, and one larger end for use in larger areas like the back and legs, to help relieve muscle tension. Reflexology wands are quite thin and have one pointed end to be used for stimulating reflex points in the ears, and one small rounded end for stimulating reflex points in the face, hands, and feet. These wands can also be used on the energy body to open chakras and direct energy.

Generators: Crystal generators are used to draw in, direct, and amplify universal energy. They may occasionally form naturally, but are more commonly cut and polished into their characteristic shape—six equal sides and six equal faces that join to form a perfect point at the top of the crystal. Many healers use generators for sending distance healing energy, amplifying the power of crystal grids, and drawing energy into a healing room or sacred space. This shape is also excellent for promoting group cooperation and for helping people work together to achieve a common goal. For more on generator crystals, see page 77.

Skulls: Crystal skulls are becoming more popular each day and offer an interesting approach to working with crystal energy. Most proponents of crystal skulls believe that there are many ancient skulls. The origins and history of these objects are hotly debated, but if you can see beyond the mystery, there is much to be learned from working with them. Most commonly, they are used for channeling. Some believe that this information comes from the skull itself, while others believe the skull is simply a portal to connect with beings from other dimensions. Many people claim that the crystal skulls are here on Earth at this time to assist with the evolution of human consciousness. They are powerful tools for enhancing meditation and healing work.

Donuts: These stones have been carved into a flat circular disc with a round hole cut out of the center. Donuts are frequently worn as necklaces by stringing them onto a cord. This shape is also known as a pi stone and is used in the ritual of the Munay-Ki rites, a shamanic practice originating in South America.

Merkaba: Sometimes referred to as a double tetrahedron or as a star tetrahedron, the merkaba displays twenty-four faces and thirty-six edges. This shape represents balance between physical and spiritual growth. It is the most powerful sacred geometry shape and is used for spiritual transformation.

Platonic solids/sacred geometry shapes: These crystals have been cut into the five Platonic solids shapes. Plato theorized that all space in the universe, both positive and negative, followed the form of one of the five sacred shapes at right.

PLATONIC SOLID SHAPES

Tetrahedron: Displays four triangular sides and six edges. Represents the fire element. Associated with confidence, motivation, and vitality.

Cube (Hexahedron): Displays six square sides and twelve edges. Represents the Earth element. Associated with grounding, stability, and protection.

Octahedron: Displays eight triangular sides and twelve edges. Represents the air element. Associated with mental clarity, problem solving, and intellect.

Dodecahedron: Displays twelve pentagonal sides and thirty edges. Represents the spirit (or ether) element. Associated with spiritual growth.

Icosahedron: Displays twenty triangular sides and thirty edges. Represents the water element. Associated with intuition, emotional balance, and psychic awareness.

CRYSTAL COLORS

Color has been scientifically proven to affect human moods and emotions. By understanding how color influences crystal energy, you will be better able to select stones for specific healing techniques, to balance the chakra centers, and to create positive emotional shifts.

You may use this information in several ways. For example, if you find yourself consistently being drawn to pink stones this may indicate that it is time for change and new beginnings, or it may indicate that you are naturally empathic and need support as you show your compassion to others. On the other hand, if you are offended or irritated by a particular color, it may indicate that you have something to work on in one of those associated areas. For example, if you really dislike the color orange, it may indicate that you need to find more emotional balance in your life or that you need to start expressing your creativity.

Alternatively, you may use these colors to help you select a crystal for yourself. If, for example, you'd like to get in touch with your spiritual aspect, then you may want to choose a violet-colored stone like amethyst or charoite to help you develop your spirituality.

The vibrations of crystals correspond to the color spectrum, or invisible waves of energy. This spectrum includes radio waves and various types of ray—infrared, ultraviolet, visible light, X-rays, and gamma rays. In the visible part of this spectrum, the colors we humans can see range from the low-frequency vibration of the color red, to the shortest wavelength and highest frequency, ultraviolet. The electromagnetic vibration of crystal energy also corresponds to this color spectrum.

According to quantum physics, everything in the Universe contains vibrational energy, whether the cells of your body, or the rippling water of a lake. These vibrational waves make up the electromagnetic spectrum. This spectrum includes radio waves, infrared, ultraviolet and visible light, X-rays, and gamma rays. In the visible part of the spectrum, the colors we humans can see range from the low frequency vibration of red, to the shortest wavelength and highest frequency, ultraviolet. The electromagnetic vibration of crystal energy also corresponds to this color spectrum.

So which colors do you prefer in your life at the moment? The general rule is that if a color makes you feel good about yourself, carrying or wearing a crystal of that color will enhance its special qualities within you.

Knowing what the different colors mean and the energy they invoke in your life means you can easily understand the basics of crystal power. For the purposes of manifestation, the following pages provide a quick rundown of the colors and how they can generally help you.

Red is the color of fire, passion, growth, impulse, power, action, courage, and love. It also signifies blood, the life force and energy that gets us moving. Red empowers, uplifts, and gets things done. It's all about action and drive; so, for example, if you are suffering from a lack of power, you may need a red crystal in your life. Red crystals include the bloodstone, with its spots of blood-like red (hence its name), intense red garnet and red carnelian, and the cooler red ruby.

Yellow is thought to be the color of communication, wisdom, joy, and happiness. It is also the color that brings clarity and a sharp mind. When yellow moves into orange, the qualities of red's warmth and mindfulness are included. Orange-yellow imparts a sense of focus, while the clean light yellow of fluorite clears the mind, making it active and alert. Use yellow or orange stones for clarity, decision-making, sharper memory, and concentration skills.

Green is the color of self-respect, well-being, and balance. It also symbolizes learning, growth, and harmony, and it is a powerful healer for vitalizing the life force. On another level, green can promote material and financial success. Green jade is a sacred stone in parts of eastern Asia, used in feng shui to promote successful business. All green crystals have the power to invoke growth, to welcome change, to pursue new ideas, or to free yourself from the demands of others.

In mystical traditions, the color **blue** has long been thought to enhance intuition, generate compassion, and invoke spiritual development. Blue crystals include those that edge towards violet and lavender blue, such as varieties of agate and tourmaline. Blue crystals all have a common theme, so it's easy to see how these crystals can work in your life.

Purple has been used to symbolize magic, mystery, and spirituality, and was once a color favored by royalty. A mixture of red (dynamic and active energy) and blue (otherworldly and intuitive), purple is a color of creativity, imagination, inspiration, and universal wisdom.

Pink crystals invoke feelings of caring, tenderness, self-worth, love, and acceptance.

Brown aligns to the color of Earth and is associated with the material or down-to-Earth side of life, connecting us to stability and encouraging acceptance of the tangible world.

White crystals (or clear crystals that have no color) are symbolic of new beginnings and development in any direction. White clears clutter and obstacles away, brings mental and spiritual clarity, and purifies thoughts and actions so you can see how to be truly fortunate.

Although **black** is not technically a color because it absorbs all light, it is still an important "energy" in the crystal kingdom. It is an energy of emptiness into which anything may emerge and disappear once again, providing a sense of potential and possibility in the future. Black gemstones have often been used as stones of prophecy. On another level, they symbolize self-control and resilience.

CHOOSING YOUR CRYSTALS

Choosing crystals for yourself is an important part of developing a personal relationship with your stones. You may be drawn to purchase or work with a stone for yourself, for a friend or family member, or even for a client if you're offering sessions professionally. There are several methods to choose between: use your logic, your intuition, or a combination of both to assist you.

Once you've purchased your selected stones, you can also use these techniques for selecting the appropriate crystal for your purpose—whether that be healing, divination, meditation, intuitive development, or personal growth.

Occasionally, you may find you feel immensely attracted to a particular crystal. This can happen when choosing a stone from your collection or when shopping for crystals. When you feel called to work with a stone, it's usually because your intuition is guiding you to what you need most. It's important to listen to this inner guidance, as there is usually a good reason for this connection. This feeling can present itself in many ways—an inner knowing to use the stone or a strong visual connection.

There will be times in your life when you know you have something important and specific to work on—such as emotional healing, repairing friendships, or manifesting prosperity. Using the known properties of stones as recorded in books such as this is a useful way of narrowing down your choices. For example, if you're feeling energetically drained and lethargic, you may need a stone for setting energetic boundaries with those who are tapping into your energy field. See Part Two for a guide to various stones and their properties. Once you have a shortlist of crystals to choose from, you can use a more intuitive method to select the right stone for your purpose. Use this method when purchasing new crystals or when selecting the appropriate stone from your collection.

Trusting the Universe

There may be times when you don't have any pressing influence on your crystal choice. When this is the case, it can be fun to ask the universe for guidance on what you need most. One of the simplest ways to do this is to choose a crystal at random from your collection. Place a mixture of tumbled stones and crystals into a bowl or small pouch and place it in front of you. Take a deep breath in, close your eyes, and ask the universe to guide you in choosing the stone that's for your highest good. Select a crystal out of the bowl or bag at random while holding your intention to choose the stone that's most needed, and carry it with you throughout the day. At the end of the day, read about the known properties of your stone. Reflect on your day and think about how those properties may have supported you or influenced events that took place.

Dreaming of Crystals

On rare occasions, you may see a crystal within your dream state. This can be a powerful message from your subconscious mind that you need to work with the energy of this particular stone. When you wake up, reflect on the experience. Make some notes in your dream journal, if you have one, or on a piece of paper, and think about how you felt emotionally when you saw the crystal, what you were doing with the stone when you came across it, whether there were any symbols or archetypes present when the stone appeared, and so on. Dream symbols may include anything that seemed to stand out in your dream—an object like a rocking chair or a book, an animal such as a swan or an elephant, or any number of letters, numbers, or traditional symbols or signs (like a peace sign or Om symbol). Archetypes may also present themselves in your dream state. Archetypes may include deities, archangels, ascended masters, or representations of the zodiacal houses or tarot arcana. These symbols and archetypes typically have strong associations that can give you clues as to the potential uses or energetic qualities of your crystals and why the stones may be important for you to use right now. If you have the stone in your collection, this may be a sign to work with it; if not, consider purchasing it.

The Om symbol is a sacred mantra that represents the totality of consciousness and all that is.

Using a Pendulum to Select a Crystal

A pendulum is an object suspended from a string that is used for reading energy and also in divination.

You can use any type of pendulum for this technique, but a quartz crystal pendulum or a copper pendulum is recommended because of their ability to amplify and conduct energy. Hold the pendulum and ask it to show you a "yes" movement, taking note of how the pendulum moves—fast or slow, clockwise or counterclockwise, back and forth, or side to side.

Repeat this process, this time asking the pendulum to show you a "no" movement. Once you're familiar with your pendulum's "yes" and "no" movements, gather a collection of stones in front of you.

Hold your pendulum over the first crystal in the group and ask aloud, "Is this the correct crystal for me to use for [your purpose] at this time?" If your pendulum answers, "yes," place the crystal aside. Repeat this process for all of the stones, setting aside any that your pendulum shows would be beneficial for you.

You may choose to use this crystal selection technique when purchasing new crystals to determine if they are right for your collection, or you can use your pendulum to help you choose the best stone for your purpose from those you already own.

Zodiac Crystals

People have been wearing and using zodiac stones for thousands of years, but in modern days, these traditional stones are often replaced with birthstones.

Birthstones are gemstones (both precious and semiprecious) that are assigned to a specific month. The modern list of birthstones was created in 1912 by the National Association of Jewelers in the USA. Many of the gemstones included in the list were loosely based on those traditionally assigned to signs of the zodiac. However, birthstones aren't as energetically aligned with your unique astrological influences as those that follow the dates of the zodiac.

Since zodiac stones have a correspondence to the planet that rules over your zodiac sign, choosing a zodiac crystal rather than a birthstone is recommended, as it will work better in energetically supporting what you need. In some cases, these stones may be the same, but this isn't always the case. Wearing or using crystals for their zodiac correspondences will amplify the positive traits of your sign while working to balance its negative traits.

There are many diverse lists of stones and crystals associated with the zodiac signs. Some say the crystal is associated with the month rather than the astrological zodiac, and these are often suggested in traditional sources, but here is my preferred list according to astrological sign.

Sign	Crystal	Keyword
Aries (March 21–April 19)	Ruby	Passionate
Taurus (April 20–May 20)	Emerald	Practical
Gemini (May 21–June 21)	Citrine	Versatile
Cancer (June 22–July 23)	Moonstone	Sensitive
Leo (July 24–August 23)	Tiger's eye	Radiant
Virgo (August 24–September 22)	Peridot	Discriminating
Libra (September 23–October 22)	Blue sapphire	Diplomatic
Scorpio (October 23–November 22)	Obsidian	Powerful
Sagittarius (November 23–December 21)	Turquoise	Adventurous
Capricorn (December 22–January 20)	Garnet	Ambitious
Aquarius (January 21–February 19)	Amber	Original
Pisces (February 20–March 20)	Amethyst	Visionary

Attraction Factor

For the beginner, and while you are learning about the power of manifestation that is in you, choose crystals that are not only in the "right" category for your intention but that also speak to you and stand out from the others. As you flick through the pages, you might come across one crystal that seems to be made for you, whatever category it is. You can simply skim through each relevant section until you spot a crystal that calls out to you. Go with your instinct. Remember, what you are attracted to is also what you can attract right now.

Attachment

The crystals described in this book are usually available in shops and online, although some may be more expensive due to their scarcity. If you can't get hold of a crystal that you feel is just right for you, don't give up on your goal. Change your focus to another more accessible crystal that will work equally well. It is all about attitude, action, and belief, and however pretty the rare crystal is or however fabulous its powers, if you can't get one now then drop the attachment and choose another. Being able to adapt and change is itself a sign to the universe that you are serious about manifesting your desire!

Receiving Crystals as Gifts

One of the most beautiful ways you can be brought together with a special stone is if it is gifted to you. Receiving a crystal as a gift amplifies the energy of the stone because it is chosen and presented with love by someone else.

When a crystal is given to you, pay special attention and reflect on why it may have been presented to you at this time in your life. It can also be useful to ask the person giving you the stone why they chose that specific crystal—their intuition may have played an important role in the selection and can give you valuable insight as to how to best utilize it.

The energy of healing crystals is one of the most sacred and beautiful gifts that you can give or receive.

CH

2

CARING FOR CRYSTALS

I f you choose to buy "tumbled stones," smaller pieces of crystal that have been turned for many hours in fine grit to give them a tough and smooth surface, they don't really need much care apart from a ritual cleansing after purchase. They can be kept in a pouch or bag as they rarely damage one another.

But many crystals are fragile, particularly those whose structure is layered or in clusters like the agates and white quartz crystals. These can easily splinter or crack, and any natural points or finely polished surfaces can scratch or chip.

Most crystals will need to be wrapped in a silk or cotton scarf or cloth to prevent scratching, and to protect against negativity, unless you are placing them in various points in the home. Always cleanse crystals after purchase, particularly jewelry, which may have been worn by someone else and may still carry their psychic footprints.

STORING YOUR CRYSTALS

Dedicate a special sacred place for your crystals, keep them safely in a pouch and carry this around with you, arrange them on a desk where you can handle them frequently, or simply wear them as jewelry. It may just be one crystal you're tuning in to, so that you can manifest something specific, but you should still make sure you care for this crystal as you would your best friend.

CLEANSING YOUR CRYSTALS

Crystals have the ability to receive, store, and transmit energy, so they should be frequently cleansed of any negative energies. People often refer to energy as being "positive" or "negative," but really there is just energy that is either beneficial for you or not. Cleansing your crystals removes energy that is not serving your highest good.

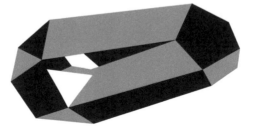

When you first bring your crystals home, the first thing you should do is to cleanse them. Gently immersing them in the sea or under running stream water—or if you don't have access to either, under a running tap—is one simple method. As you do so, affirm in your mind or out loud that all negativity will be washed away, and positive energy will permeate the crystal. You can also leave the crystal on a window ledge for three days and nights in a row to recharge its energy from both the sun's and moon's light.

Many crystals become dust collectors simply because we leave them lying around on ledges and forget them. Please don't do this, as they won't ever help you to manifest anything, except more dust! (Do you leave your friends to sit on a ledge and get dusty?) Remember to talk to them as you would your best friend. Also touch them, handle them, or take them out with you when you go somewhere special.

The ritual of washing crystals cleanses them of negative energy picked up on their journey to you.

If you work with a crystal regularly, it should be cleansed before and after use. Crystals that you wear in jewelry or carry with you but which you don't use for specific techniques should be cleansed about once a week. It's always best to use your inner guidance when determining how frequently to cleanse your stones. If you feel that the crystal is not working as well as it previously did, it likely needs to be cleansed. Similarly, if you have a particularly difficult day (physically, emotionally, or spiritually), you should cleanse this energy from your stone right away. The same guidelines apply if you encounter "negativity" from other people or your environment.

There are many techniques you can use to cleanse your crystals, but with so many options available, choosing one can feel overwhelming. Your intuition can play an important role in helping you select the cleansing method that's right for you and your particular crystal, so you should listen to your inner guidance. However, there are also some important tips to be aware of before diving in and performing some of the common cleansing techniques.

Set an intention for clearing energy: No matter which cleansing method you choose, it's beneficial to hold the intention to cleanse the crystal and remove all energy from the stone that isn't for the highest good of your being. You should also intend to transmute any negative energy that's released from the crystal into positive energy for the highest good of all.

Transmute negative energy: When cleansing your crystals, it is very important that you transmute the negative energy that is released from your stone into positive energy so that the negativity does not accumulate in your space. Visualization is the simplest and most effective method of transmuting negativity. As you perform any of the following cleansing techniques, visualize the energy being released from your stone and see it surrounded by bright white light. See this white light shine brighter, and watch it begin to break apart and dissolve the negativity released from your stone. See the negativity completely dissipate, leaving nothing in your space. Then visualize your crystal surrounded with the pink light of love and positivity. See this light expand and fill your space, pushing out any remaining negativity and transforming it into positive, loving energy.

CRYSTAL CLEANSING METHODS

Water: Water has been known as a cleansing agent for thousands of years. Clearing negative energy from stones with water is a common practice. There are several ways to do this. The most common method involves holding the crystals in your hands and placing them beneath running water. You may also choose to fill a bowl with water and soak your stones overnight. Some people prefer to cleanse their stones in a pond or lake, river or stream, or even in the ocean, as they feel it is a more natural form of water cleansing. Using water can be a little messy and rather inconvenient if you need to cleanse a large quantity of crystals. Additionally, some crystals can actually be damaged by water. Soft or friable stones are most prone to water damage—including angelite, celestite, selenite, calcite, ulexite, turquoise, azurite, kyanite, and more. For this reason, water is not typically recommend as a frequent cleansing method. However, using water to physically clean dusty or grimy stones can be beneficial.

Water is the most common cleansing method, but it isn't safe for all crystals.

Smudging: Smudging is the art of burning sacred herbs and using the purifying smoke for cleansing. It is a practice that's been in existence for thousands of years and is most commonly associated with the Native American peoples of North America who use herbs such as sage, sweetgrass, cedar, and others for purification. To smudge your crystals, burn one of these herbs, or palo santo (a sacred wood from South America, easy to come by in most New Age stores), in a fireproof container, such as an abalone shell or ceramic dish, and pass your crystal through the smoke. Hold the crystal in the smoke until you intuitively feel the energy is free of anything negative or unwanted. This cleansing method is convenient for cleansing large quantities of stones, but it may be problematic if used in a space with fragrance-sensitive or asthmatic people.

Sound vibration: Sound is an intensely purifying energy and its vibration has been used for driving away negative energy by cultures across the globe. From drums to gongs, chimes, or even singing bowls, these instruments emit powerful, cleansing sound vibrations. Place your crystal or a group of stones on a tabletop or in your sacred space and sound the instrument several times. Continue sounding the instrument for at least thirty seconds, or until you intuitively feel a shift in the energy of your stones.

You can even try placing your crystals within a singing bowl—a metallic bowl, frequently of Tibetan (region of China) origin, that is used for meditation and space clearing—to cleanse them. It can be gonged using a stick, or the rim of the bowl can be rubbed with the stick to produce an intense, cleansing sound vibration. However, if placing stones within the bowl, you should be careful with rough stones because the vibration of the bowl could chip them. Some singing bowls are even made from quartz crystal. These are much louder and more intense than the metal singing bowls and combine the energy of the sound vibration with the amplifying capability of quartz crystal.

Cleansing visualization: Your intention is one of the most powerful cleansing methods available, but only if you're confident in your ability to direct and focus energy. This is a simple and convenient cleansing technique because it doesn't require any supplies or materials. Simply hold your crystal, or a few crystals, in your hands. Close your eyes, take a deep breath, and slowly exhale. Visualize drawing universal healing light into the top of your head. See this light enter your body and move out of your hands and into the stone. Feel the energy surround the crystal and move into it, cleansing it of any low-frequency vibrations. In your mind's eye, see the crystal glow with divine light until you intuitively feel that the energy has shifted, dissolving any negativity or unwanted energy. When you intuitively feel that the stone has been cleared, stop the visualization.

You can easily adapt this exercise for a large quantity of crystals by holding your hands above them and projecting the energy from your hands to all of the crystals in the group. This is one of the safest and most effective cleansing methods, one where you need not be concerned about breaking or ruining your stones.

FIRE, EARTH, AIR, AND WATER RITUAL

Another way to cleanse and re-energize your crystals is by using this ritual. The energy of the four elements brings the crystal into harmony with your wishes and desires.

YOU WILL NEED:
- Your crystal(s)
- A white candle
- A bowl of spring water
- A piece of paper and pen

WHAT TO DO:

1 Write down the name or names of your new crystals on the piece of paper in a list (they can be in any order) and place the stones alongside their names. This action represents the element of Air, which is associated with naming things. Words are magical, and as soon as we invoke the crystal by naming it aloud, we are bringing it to life in our own world.

2 Now gaze at the crystals on your paper and try to visualize them surrounded by golden light from the core of the Earth, cleansing, energizing, and nurturing them. As you gaze at them, name them one by one, repeating their names again and again at least ten times. This is the Earth ritual.

3 Now light the candle, and take each crystal in turn and pass it slowly through the top of the candle flame—being careful not to burn yourself. This is how you cleanse and energize a stone by Fire.

4 Next, for the Water ritual, place the crystals on the table in a circle next to the bowl of water. If you have only one or two crystals, place them in the center of the table. Touch each stone in turn with a drop of water on your finger. As you do so, say the following for each crystal: "Crystal friend, you are now cleansed and purified."

5 Finally, thank the crystals for being there for you and then blow out the candle. Your crystals are now ready to be dedicated and/or programmed (see Chapter 3).

CH

3

CRYSTAL ENERGY

Learning to sense the subtle energy of crystals is an important part of working with your stones. Developing this energetic sensitivity helps you to connect with your intuition as well as enhancing your personal relationship with your crystals. The powerful energy of your stones can help you learn to tune into the universe around you. If you've struggled with sensing energy in the past, practicing the following techniques will help you to feel the energy of your crystals.

The first step to learning to sense crystal energy is to discover which is your sending hand and which is your receiving. Although some ambidextrous people can sense energy equally in both hands, most people find they have one hand in which they feel energy more strongly. Typically, your receiving hand is your nondominant hand and it draws in universal energy. Your sending hand is your dominant hand (the hand with which you write) and moves energy out of the body and back out to the universe after the receiving hand has drawn it in. The process of sending and receiving energy is constant, but you can also consciously direct the energy flow, during healing and meditation, for example.

SENSING ENERGY

A simple way to become familiar with energy is to learn to sense your own. Start by rubbing the palms of your hands together to activate the tiny energy centers located here. Then draw your hands apart and slowly move them together, palms facing one another, until you feel the quality of the energy shift or change. Continue moving your hands together and apart to become familiar with the feeling of your energy.

After becoming familiar with your own energy field, you can introduce a crystal. Hold a quartz crystal in one hand while performing the technique above. Notice any subtle differences in the way the energy feels—this is the energy of the crystal.

If you find it difficult to feel the energy of the crystal in this way, hold a quartz crystal point in your dominant hand and point it toward the palm of your receiving hand. The energy in a quartz crystal moves from the base of the crystal toward the point. The termination, or point, should be about one to two inches from your palm. Begin drawing small clockwise circles with the crystal above your palm. Try to tune in and feel the energy where the circles are being drawn. You can also try moving the crystal point closer to your hand, then further away; note how this changes the sensation. Try making the circles larger or smaller, or even reversing the direction. How do the temperature, density, sensation change as you move the crystal in different ways? You may find it useful to make some notes about this in your crystal affrmation journal (see page 71).

Crystals have the ability to amplify energy, so they are powerful when used to help you sense subtle energy.

COLOR AND ENERGY

Another great way to start getting familiar with the subtle differences in crystal energy is to tune into the color vibration of your stones. Calcite crystals work well for this technique as they come in a wide variety of colors. Gather an assortment of at least three different-colored calcite stones and place them on the table in front of you. Pick up the first stone and hold it in your hands. Take a deep breath in, close your eyes, and tune into the stone's energy. After a few minutes, open your eyes, and set the stone down. Repeat the exercise with each stone, noticing the changes in energy caused by the different colors. Perhaps make some notes about this in your crystal affirmation journal.

The visible color of all minerals is created by the way that light reflects within the stone's internal surfaces.

DEDICATING YOUR CRYSTALS

Once you have your crystal in your possession, you need to dedicate it, with the intention that only positive energy will flow through it, and it is only going to be used for the good of all. This dedication will focus all the goodness of the universe into the crystal, and also purges any negative energy that may have already been attached to the stone, whether from it being handled by others, or from any geopathic stress that permeated the crystal during its formation deep within the Earth's surface.

Although crystals absorb and neutralize negative energy, turning it into positive energy, these outside influences can become ghostly hangers-on if the stone hasn't been used or treated with love or care for some time. Often stones hang around in shops or are in transit and don't take kindly to being treated like poor cattle on their way to market! So it's important to dedicate your crystals to positive healing energies to protect them from any other negative influences in the future, too.

When dedicating your crystals to positive healing energy, you will find that you begin to feel an affinity for the stone in question. Always make sure that you use the crystal only for the power of goodness and not to cause bad influences on anyone, including yourself.

1 Sit down in a quiet place with the crystal cupped in your hands. Close your eyes and focus on your breathing, taking deep, slow, regular breaths. Make sure your feet are both flat on the floor, preferably without shoes, so that you are grounded and feel a connection to the Earth.

2 In your mind, imagine you are like a tree, rooted to the ground, and from your feet a golden light begins to rise up through you, until its warmth fills every cell of your body. As it spreads throughout you it then enters the crystal, filling it with harmony and heat from the very depths of the Earth.

3 Now visualize a ray of pure white light beaming down from above, as if it has come from the galaxies and the universe. As this light envelops you it merges with the golden warmth so you and the crystal are both protected, nurtured, and filled with positive energy.

4 Next, say this dedication either aloud or in your mind: "This crystal will only be used for the highest good."

5 Now open your eyes and gaze at your stone while repeating the dedication to the crystal five times and ending with the words, "So mote it be."

You can also dedicate your stone to a specific entity who protects and guides you, such as a deity, saint, guardian angel, or spirit guide. Once you have completed your dedication, you will find yourself more in tune with your crystal's powers. You are now ready to program it.

Many healers believe that the act of dedication helps to awaken the deva, or spirit, of the stone, and that it creates a sacred contract with this deva that you will use the crystal with integrity and positive purpose. By awakening the crystal deva, it will be easier for you to connect with the energy of the stone. This in turn will help you develop your personal relationship with your crystal and enhance the intuitive insight you receive.

CRYSTALLINE CONSCIOUSNESS

Many healers think of crystal devas as living beings, but for others, it's difficult to think of crystals as having a consciousness of their own. When thinking about crystal consciousness in terms of the deva, most people visualize a small, fairylike spirit living within the stone. In a similar way, some people picture the consciousness of human beings as a tiny person controlling the mind and body from inside of the head.

Crystal devas were known as stone spirits to many ancient peoples. In many cultures, these spirits were considered to be guides that created connections between human consciousness and crystal energy, allowing the user to receive healing, wisdom, and protection from the stone. Some modern healers attribute the healing properties of specific stones to their associated crystal deva.

After dedicating your stones, the next step is to show your gratitude to the crystal spirits by thanking the stones for working with you. The simplest way to do this is to speak your message aloud, thanking the stone for sharing its energy with you and for working with you for healing and balance. This message can be short and sweet or as elaborate as you like. The most important thing is to be sincere—send feelings of love and gratitude to the crystal and intent to strengthen your connection to the stone.

Regardless of whether or not you feel your crystal is a living being, has a consciousness, or is just an object possessing energy, treat this tool of light with respect. Crystals should be honored and thanked for their gifts and their amazing healing abilities.

MANIFESTATION

We all want to make our dreams come true or just make something specific happen. We wish on stars, throw coins in a fountain, believe in luck or fate. But most of us never really empower ourselves with the very essence of manifestation—being at one with not only ourselves, but also the universe within us. The great news is that with the help of your crystal friends you can start to find this sense of oneness and manifest your dreams and goals. Be warned, it takes willingness, intention, goodness, gratitude, effort, passion, and, most of all, self-belief. Manifestation is about letting the universe within you reveal itself through you and your unique identity and desires. But to manifest your dreams you have to really know yourself and what you truly want, or rather what you actually seek. And with that knowledge, you must know how to call on the universal energy within you to make your life complete.

The word "manifest" derives from the Latin word *manifestus*, meaning clear, apparent, or proved by direct evidence. In other words, whether you have a dream of an abundant lifestyle, a yearning for a house in the country, or a wish for a happy family, you have to make it "real." We can only make these dreams come true (or bring them into tangible reality) if we are ready to cast off expectations, conditions, assumptions, and emotional poisons—to cut to the core and reveal our true self. This self is the one that lies deep within us, profoundly linked to our soul's purpose and its connection to the universe. In fact, the universe lies within us, just as it appears to lie without us. It is only once we start to really believe this, and by "believe," I mean "know and experience" this, that can we actually manifest that which we desire.

WANTS AND NEEDS

Wanting and needing are two very different things. "Want" implies a lack. When we are "wanting" it is because we don't have whatever it is we think we lack. We feel a sense of missing out—or we feel inadequate in some way because we don't "own" this thing, or quality of life. We may be envious of others who are wealthy or in happy marriages, and so we feel we deserve those things and ought to have them in our own lives. But whether the things we want on the surface are in tandem with what our soul or deeper purpose has intended for us is another matter. This is not about "fate," it is about innate potential and what we truly seek. This is when we have to learn to accept every piece of goodness that we do get, and also learn to let go and trust in the flow of the universe, letting goodness come to us.

When we feel we need a change of scenery, new shoes, or to be loved, we are also expressing a sense of lack. But this time it is about necessity—in other words, it is necessary for us to have that thing to make us feel at one with ourselves. It seems essential to our very existence. But, as with wanting, we have to be careful we aren't getting carried away with cultural or family expectations about what we need. Both "want" and "need" are feelings we attach ourselves to throughout life. It is only when we give and receive with no emotional investment—only emotional involvement, enjoying the giving or accepting, observing or being aware of our reactions—that we can really manifest that which we are truly blessed to have.

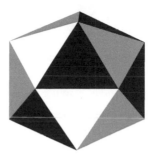

Principles of Manifestation

The principles of manifestation can be divided into seven steps, and, before you start to use crystals to reinforce and amplify your intentions, it's important that you are seeing things objectively. You need to be aware of what it is you truly seek, clear of all emotional and mental negativity, and open, serene, and ready for working with the power of your crystal friends.

1 Self-Awareness
2 Knowing What You Truly Seek Right Now
3 Affirmations and Intention
4 Belief and Passion
5 Creative Engagement
6 Timing and Realistic Goals
7 Letting Go, Acceptance, and Gratitude

Once you have realized how serious it is to think, feel, and imagine yourself having the things you truly desire—and you are sure that you know what your current intention is—then you can begin to work with the crystals of your choice.

PROGRAMMING YOUR CRYSTALS

Crystals can be programmed so that their energy is focused on something specific and so that your intention is reinforced by the crystal's own power. Once a stone has been programmed, it will continually work with that desire until it is cleared or reprogrammed.

Although one crystal can convey, say, two or three intentions at the same time, it's important that they are compatible. In other words, if you seek new romance, but also wish to forget a past love affair, it would be wise to use two different crystals for these two very different desires.

Of course, you can just program your crystals for general themes such as for healing, protection, or spiritual guidance. You might wish for more love or prosperity, or to improve your home or work environment.

Before programming your crystals, write down a list of what you want to manifest or change in your life. When you come to practice the following ritual, you will find it's easier to select specific stones.

1 Make sure you know exactly what your best intentions for the crystal
   are. Be specific and precise with your thoughts or words. If you want to
   find a new career or job, then describe exactly what kind of work you
   are seeking.

2 Select a stone that resonates to the desire. Make sure it is exactly the
   right crystal for your purpose. For example, if you are looking for peace
   and calm, choose a crystal that is already used as a meditational aid, such
   as selenite. If you want to stimulate action or to bring positive results
   quickly, select an energizing red stone, such as red carnelian, garnet, or
   ruby. For better communication choose a yellow stone, such as citrine.

3 Sit quietly with the crystal in the palm of your hand, and think about
   your desire. Keep repeating this desire or intention over and over, aloud
   or in your head.

4 Gaze at the crystal and relax as you feel the energy of the crystal in
   harmony with you. Now repeat your desire several times out loud to fix it
   to the crystal. You will intuitively feel when the programming is complete.

Once a stone has been programmed, depending on its purpose, wear the stone, carry it in your pocket, or place it by your bed. It can also be beneficial to hold the crystal and repeat your intentions several times a day.

Keep any specifically programmed crystals out of contact with others, to avoid them being contacted by other energies and vibrations that may disturb your own program. Protect the crystal by wrapping it in silk or cotton when not in use.

If you decide you don't need the desire, or it has been fulfilled, to de-program the crystal simply sit comfortably with the crystal in your hand and say: "All that I desired is no longer my intention; crystal, be as you once were."

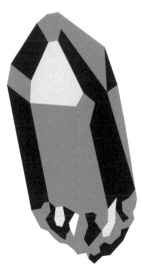

CRYSTALS AND THE CHAKRAS

Crystals are often used to restore balance to the chakras (a Sanskrit word, meaning "wheels"). The chakras are epicenters of invisible energy believed to flow around and through the body. Likened to whirlwinds or spirals of air that vibrate at different frequencies, they form an invisible interface connecting our personal body energy and the chi, or cosmic energy, which flows through all things. The chakras also correspond to the energy of seven colors.

By wearing specific gemstones for each chakra, you can increase your energy levels and enhance your manifestation powers. The chakra colors are red, orange, yellow, green, blue, indigo, and violet. If the chakras are not balanced, or if the energies are blocked, you may find you have negative thoughts or become physically tired or depressed. When the chakras are functioning normally, each will automatically respond to the particular energies needed from the universal energy field.

Aligning specific crystals with the chakras brings about harmony and well-being, and a sense of what truly matters to you.

The nine chakras are as follows:

The Base or Root Chakra: The base chakra is located at the base of the spine. This chakra is concerned with our sense of being "grounded."

The Sacral Chakra: Located approximately a hand's breadth below the navel, the sacral chakra is concerned with our sex drive, creativity, and emotional state.

The Solar Plexus Chakra: Situated between the navel and the breastbone, the third chakra is the seat of personal power. Rather like having one's own inner "sun," it gives us a strong ego, a sense of our own personal character, individuality, and willpower.

The Heart Chakra: Situated behind the breastbone and in front of the spine, the heart chakra vibrates to the colors green and pink, and is the center of warm, loving feelings. This chakra is about true compassion, love, and spirituality.

The Throat Chakra: The throat chakra is located in the lower end of the throat and is the center for thought, communication, music, speech, and writing.

The Third Eye Chakra: Located in the center of the brow, the third eye vibrates to the color indigo and is concerned with inspiration, imagination, and psychic ability.

The Crown Chakra: Situated on the top of the head, this is the center for true spirituality and enlightenment. It allows for the inward flow of wisdom and brings the gift of cosmic consciousness.

Palm Chakras: In the center of each palm are the chakras for "exchanging" energy. Here we give and receive, offer and accept, and so on. Here we hold crystals to empower us and connect us to the universal energy flow.

For more on the associations between chakras and crystals, see Chapter 5.

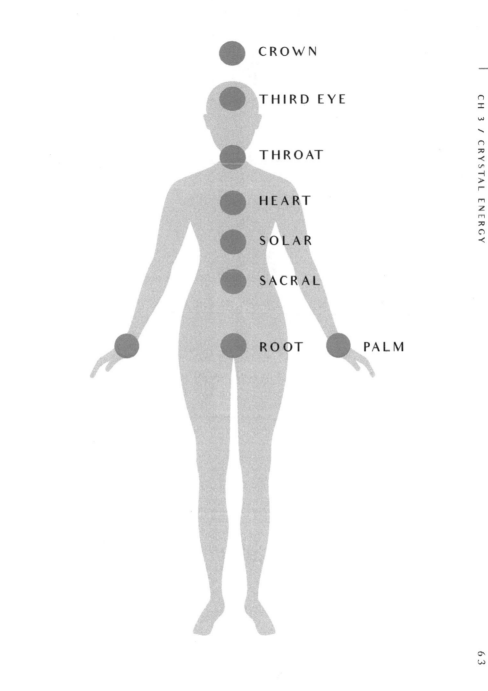

CROWN

THIRD EYE

THROAT

HEART

SOLAR

SACRAL

ROOT   PALM

CH

4

USING CRYSTALS

I t's time for you to start your exciting journey into the world of crystals and energy healing. Working with crystals is a subjective and deeply personal experience. Each person will use their stones in different ways. There are no right or wrong answers when it comes to crystal healing—there is only your experience. Work to stay present in the moment and be open to your experiences with your stones. Remember to stay focused and allow yourself to fully open up and connect with the many unique members of the mineral kingdom.

There are many ways to use crystals in your day-to-day life. You can carry a selection of stones with you in your pocket or a small pouch, or you can wear your healing stones set in jewelry. Alternatively, place a small bag (or a dish or bowl) of stones in a prominent area of your home or workplace—or anywhere you spend a great deal of time. You may choose to create a small crystal grid or a geometric arrangement of stones, or add some special crystals to a sacred stone medicine pouch.

You can also carry out some basic energy healing by placing a stone on one of your chakra centers for five to ten minutes. This will allow you to absorb the balanced, healing energy of the stone into the chakra. Perform this technique as often as you like.

CRYSTAL MEDITATION

Another way to dive deep with your healing stones is to tune into their energy during a meditation session. The following meditation can help you clear your mind and prepare for your new journey. This meditation works best when using clear quartz, rainbow fluorite, or golden tiger's eye stones because of their association with focus and mental clarity, but you can choose any crystal that you are intuitively drawn to.

1   Make yourself comfortable in a place where you will not be disturbed. Hold your crystal in cupped hands, close your eyes, and take a deep breath. Focus your attention on the stone in your hands; try to feel its energetic vibration.

2   Take a deep breath in, hold for a count of three, and slowly exhale. On your next breath, become aware of the crystal energy on a deeper level. Stay focused only on your crystal and your breathing. If you catch your mind starting to wander, return your attention to your breath. Take a deep breath in, hold for a count of three, and slowly exhale.

3   Continue in this way, allowing yourself to absorb the energy of the stone, feeling your mind focus on the present moment and releasing all other thoughts. Feel any distractions slipping away until you are only aware of yourself and your healing stone. Remain in silent meditation for as long as you like, then when you feel ready, take a deep breath in, exhale, open your eyes, and return to present-moment consciousness. Take a look around, allowing yourself to see what surrounds you but without allowing it to take your attention away from your connection to your crystal.

As you continue to practice, your goal should be to come out of the meditation and remain free from distraction for longer and longer periods of time. Eventually, you will be able to apply this disciplined approach to tuning into crystal energy under any circumstances.

CRYSTALS IN YOUR SACRED SPACE

Your sacred space is your personal sanctuary and it provides a place where you can connect to the universal source energy so that you're able to recharge and rejuvenate yourself. It may include objects that are sacred to you and your connection to the spirit, such as statues, symbols, color energy, crystals, candles and incense, and uplifting artwork. Your sacred space is a place of personal power and strength for you, and your point of connection to universal energy, so whatever you choose, it is important the items are personal and meaningful to you. Think about the ways that you'll use this sacred space and what would best support you, and choose your items and crystals accordingly. Then, as your intention changes and grows, you can update the items

The creation of a crystal altar is a simple way to pull all of these elements together in one small, convenient space. Choose an area within your sacred space where you will be able to stop and appreciate your altar regularly. It's wonderful if you can have a small desk or table to use for your altar, but a tiny shelf or even a windowsill is fine. Be sure to set an intention for your altar—what is your purpose for creating it? What would you like to use it for? Once you have a purpose in mind, choosing what to add to it becomes much easier.

You can bring some color energy (see page 26) into the space with the crystals you display, or incorporate colorful tablecloths and fabric to call in the properties associated with the colors you choose. Additionally, you can add things that are sacred to you—family heirlooms, statues, symbols, candles, incense, etc. You may also want to add something that is really sacred or beautiful to you like fresh flowers, feathers, or other objects you find in nature.

The most important part of your crystals altar is, of course, the crystals themselves, chosen according to the properties you'd like to call into your life. By referring to the information in Part Two, you can select those most relevant to you and your intentions. You can arrange the crystals in any way that you find pleasing, or you can further boost the energy of your stones by creating a crystal grid like the one opposite, which uses selenite, rhodochrosite, and blue lace agate for shielding and protection.

Crystal grids are created by arranging crystals in sacred geometric patterns. Crystal grids can fill a space with transformative healing energy, or they can be used to send distance-healing energy to people and places across the globe.

Some healers also choose to use crystal divination tools on their crystal altars. You may want to add a crystal ball, gemstone pendulum, or casting stones. When you're at your altar in your sacred space, your energy is focused and centered and allows you to clearly receive any messages that come through during your divination session.

Finally, it's recommended that you keep a selenite crystal in your sacred space. Selenite is one of the best crystals for space clearing, and keeping one atop your altar or in your space will help keep the energy free from negativity as well as calling in your guides and angels to keep the space protected.

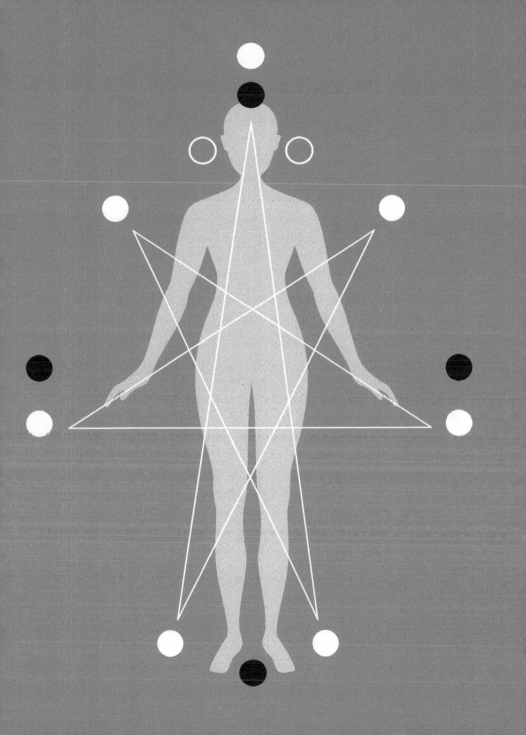

THE POWER OF CRYSTALS
AND AFFIRMATIONS

Crystals are powerful, natural amplifiers of energy. When you combine them with the transformative abilities of affirmations, you have a winning recipe for positive transformation. Affirmations are conscious statements of your intent that help to co-create your reality. They are like messages that you share with the universe in order to communicate your wants, needs, goals, dreams, vision, wishes, and desires. When you focus your full attention on manifesting your affirmation statements into being, and you support that energy with crystals, you can create major shifts in your life energy.

Some people practice the technique of programming their stones for specific purposes. Although this would seem to make sense at first, you may find this method to be a little restrictive when compared to using affirmations.

Programming your crystals (see page 58) gives them a specific and direct objective. When you program a stone, you're directing it to focus on only that one specific thing and nothing else. With affirmations, however, you're making a request of the crystal about what feels most important to you, without restricting the stone's abilities in any way. The crystal will often know best how to help you, and by working with affirmations rather than programming, you allow the crystal the freedom to work for your highest good rather than imposing your will on the stone. This is important because you may not always be able to see what is best for you or be aware of everything that's going on within your body, mind, and spirit, and the stone will work objectively on all areas of your being.

CREATING A CRYSTAL AFFIRMATION JOURNAL

Using an affirmation journal is a simple way to incorporate affirmations into your daily practice, a place where you can keep track of your affirmations and manifesting work. The journal can be used for keeping records of the transformation and change you've been able to create in your life with each affirmation.

You can create your own by choosing a blank journal, one that will keep you excited and motivated to use it. You may also want to decorate your journal to add some positive energy and personal touches to it.

Once you have your affirmation journal ready, the next step is to craft your first affirmation. Writing this affirmation states your intention to the universe and is a catalyst for personal transformation. Be sure to write your affirmation as clearly and concisely as possible, phrasing it in the present tense, as if you have already manifested it, rather than using the future tense. Stating "I will" or "I am going to" in your affirmations continues to push your manifestation of these things into the future rather than calling them into the present moment. By using the present tense, you are telling the universe that you are holding space for these things in your life and that you are ready to accept them now.

It's also important that your affirmation is framed in the positive, focusing on what you want to draw into your life, rather than focused on the negative. For example, rather than stating, "I don't want to be sick anymore," which focuses on illness, you should say something like, "My body is healthy and balanced," which focuses on overall health and wellbeing. Instead of, "I am healing the emotional pain caused by my divorce," which is full of hurtful memories and emotions, you should phrase your affirmation to read something like, "I gratefully accept new, healthy, loving relationships into my life," which is specific about what you'd like to call into being.

If you've written your affirmation to read something like, "I am not poor and no longer struggle financially," then you're placing your energy and attention on financial troubles rather than on abundance. A better solution would be to affirm that "I manifest abundance in all areas of my life including financial abundance, an abundance of love, and an abundance of good health." In this way, you shift your mindset from one of scarcity and poverty consciousness to an abundance mindset that calls in positive energy in all aspects of your life and enhances your ability to magnify that which you need most.

In this way, you manifest positive things into your life, rather than focusing your energy and intention on things that are not for your highest good. It is also recommended that you add the words, "This, or something better," to the end of your affirmation so as not to limit your manifesting potential. If you need some inspiration, you may find it useful to hold your favorite crystal while writing your affirmation. Think about the way the crystal makes you feel and about all of the ways in which you could be more aligned with positivity in your life, then craft your intention statement.

Using Your Affirmation Journal

To begin using your affirmation journal, choose a crystal that's aligned with the purpose of your affirmation. Hold the crystal in your hands and speak your affirmation aloud. Feel the energy of the stone amplifying the power of your words, sending them out with focus and direction. This act creates a positive, energetic shift in your body, mind, and spirit. You can follow this process as often as you like, but making time at least once a week to stay active with your manifesting work shows the universe that you are holding space in your life for the change to take place.

Each week when you repeat the process, take some time to jot down a few notes about how you've moved closer to manifesting things relating to your affirmation. For example, if your affirmation is focused on manifesting good health, then write about any steps you've taken to improve this aspect of your life—perhaps include some notes about your sleep habits, your diet, any visits to your doctor, or general notes about how you've been feeling. Make an assessment about whether you feel you've improved, stayed the same, or if you've gotten a bit off track. If you haven't improved since your last entry, ponder on why this might be and what you can do during the next week that will help you.

You can also record any feelings or ideas relating to this area of your life. Hold your chosen crystal while reflecting on your week and allow the energy of the stone to help shine some light on how you're connecting to the transformative energy you're creating with your affirmation. As you go through this process each week, evaluate your affirmation to be sure it's still relevant to what you'd like to manifest into your life. If, over time, your manifesting goals change, be sure to write a new affirmation and choose a new stone to work with so that you are working toward things that are aligned with the transformation you'd like to create in your life.

Be sure to date each entry in your affirmation journal so that you keep track of your growth and progress toward manifesting your affirmation. The other benefit of dating these entries is that it shows you how frequently you're actually using your journal. It can also be easy to put off the things that you likely need to do the most, so check over your entries frequently to be sure you're staying on track with a regular routine.

Because combining crystals and affirmations is such a powerful practice, it's strongly suggested that you find additional ways to incorporate this technique into your life. You may try posting your affirmations on your vision board (a visual reminder of things you'd like to manifest in your life) or even chanting your affirmation during a crystal meditation (see page 66). You can create a crystal grid, a geometric formation of crystals used for manifesting (see page 68), and place your affirmation at its center to add some extra energy to your manifesting practice. Or try writing your affirmation on a piece of paper and wrapping it around your crystal to charge it with the vibration of your intention. Carry this stone with you wherever you go to work on your manifesting.

CREATING A CRYSTAL MEDICINE POUCH

The use of crystal medicine pouches, or mojo bags, goes back thousands and thousands of years. These bags are small pouches filled with crystals and sacred objects that are used to enhance personal power, intuitive guidance, healing, spirit connection, and protective energy.

In your medicine pouch you can include things like healing stones, feathers, shells, or other objects that are meaningful to you. It's wonderful if the objects correspond to a specific purpose or intention for your medicine bag—such as love, prosperity, intuitive development, and so on.

Choosing Crystals for Your Medicine Pouch

The crystals in your medicine bag amplify your purpose and intention. You can choose these crystals intuitively or based on their known properties. Just be sure to select stones related to your purpose. Choosing each crystal within your medicine pouch adds a personalized touch to the healing energy you're cultivating. This collection of stones can then be used to support, comfort, and empower you as you create major life change and transformation. After selecting your crystals, you should cleanse them and add them to the pouch.

Empowering Your Medicine Pouch

After you have added all of your chosen cleansed stones to your bag, you can empower your medicine pouch. Make yourself comfortable in your sacred space and empty all of the objects from your pouch. Place the pouch in front of you and pick up the first object. Hold it in your hands and think about the reason you've chosen to include it in your bag. Put the item inside your bag while focusing on this intention. Continue with this practice for each item until you have placed all of the objects back in the bag. When everything is within the pouch, hold it in your hands and visualize it being surrounded by universal healing light.

Adding special objects to your medicine pouch, like feathers or family heirlooms, personalizes it.

Using Your Crystal Pouch

Once you've empowered your crystal medicine pouch, it's ready for you to wear or carry with you. You can wear it as part of your daily crystal routine or use it only on special occasions. When you're not actively using your medicine bag, it's best to keep it in your sacred space or on your altar.

Cleansing Your Medicine Pouch

It's important to routinely cleanse your medicine pouch to keep its energy pure and high frequency. You can cleanse the entire pouch at once; there's no need to cleanse each item individually. You can smudge your medicine bag, cleanse it with sound vibration, or place it in the moonlight overnight.

Your medicine bag can be made from any material, but most healers prefer natural materials like leather or silk.

Updating Your Medicine Pouch

As time passes and your life shifts and changes, you may need to update the contents of your medicine pouch. As you grow and change personally, the items in your bag should be changed to match what you want to draw into your life. Trust your intuition as to when to update the items. Remember, you'll need to empower the bag and its contents again after changing any of the items within it.

You can cleanse and charge your medicine pouch by placing it on your windowsill in the moonlight overnight.

SETTING UP A GENERATOR CRYSTAL

Before you begin working with the crystals suggested in Part Two, it's useful to set up a generator crystal. This is a power source, a focal crystal that amplifies your intentions, as well as the positive effects of the other crystals used in your work. You can leave this set up on a special altar or sacred space, to continually amplify placements of crystals around the home. But where should you put it?

In the Chinese art of feng shui, the southeast corner of your home is highly important for attracting wealth. But you may be seeking other forms of abundance, such as love, a fulfilling home life, spiritual happiness, or a successful business. On page 78 is a diagram of the nine other areas of your home that correspond to different qualities you may be seeking. Set up your generator crystal and/or sacred space or altar (you can dress a table with flowers, candles, souvenirs, and so on to make it special) in the part of your home that corresponds to your current goal. This will amplify your intention to the universe.

Each of the eight compass points corresponds to specific energies in feng shui. For example, if you are seeking new romance, set up your generator crystal in the southwest corner of your home to boost its power.

YOU WILL NEED:
- A sunny day
- A clear quartz crystal (either in the shape of a large terminated point, or a cluster of points radiating outward from the base)
- An altar, table, or sacred space in the preferred corner of your home
- Two white candles

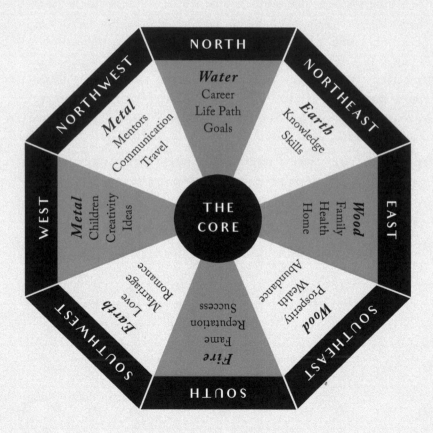

WHAT TO DO:

1 After you have cleansed your crystal (see page 41) take it outside into the sun. If you don't have outdoor space, take the crystal to a peaceful park, quiet bit of the countryside, or beach. Stand for a few moments, eyes closed, facing toward the sun with the crystal in your hands.

2 Feel the energy of the crystal in your hands as it aligns with the solar power and repeat, in your mind or out loud, the following spell: "With this crystal all good intentions will be fired with the light of the sun and the blessing of the universe. I thank you for helping me to manifest my desire."

3 Now open your eyes and return to your altar.

4 Place the crystal between two white candles. Light the two candles and then again place your hands around the crystal, repeating the following: "With this crystal all good intentions will be fired with the power of the universe. I am at one, so all that I seek will be inspired."

5 Sit for a few moments absorbing the energy from the crystal between your hands. Then, when you are ready, let go and blow out the candles.

6 Leave the crystal in its place and occasionally perform the same generator exercise to boost your manifestation powers before using other spells, placements, or grids.

CONNECTING TO THE CREATIVE FORCE OF THE UNIVERSE

Make a commitment (now!) to do this simple meditational exercise every day. It doesn't have to be for long—maybe three to five minutes at a time. In the silent place you will create with this practice, where everything is connected with everything else, you will feel at one with the unlimited power of creative imagination.

Once you practice this on a regular basis, you'll notice what seems like new flashes of insight about what you are seeking. In fact, these flashes of insight are within you, but have been relegated to the unconscious part of your mind. Most of your thought processes may be taken up with negative thinking or worry, doubt, fear, or attending to what has to be done in the here and now. But after practicing meditation, you'll find the deeper insights of your mind flow up to your consciousness. Free from tangled thoughts and complexes, and with this new creative awareness, you will realize what it is you really seek, and can start to manifest it.

1 Relax, and find somewhere quiet and comfortable to sit. With your eyes closed, become aware of your breathing. Take slow breaths, in and out, until you feel calm and peaceful. Concentrate on your breathing.

2 Imagine each breath is like a door opening and closing. As you breathe in you are letting in beautiful thoughts and ideas. When you breathe out you are releasing dull or meaningless ones. As you breathe in, imagine the smell of roses, the smell of baked bread, or the sight of your favorite friend. As you breathe out, imagine that you're decluttering your home. You're chucking out those unwanted nicknacks, clothes you never wear, and magazines you never read. When you breathe out, all negative thoughts, fears, or self-doubt leave too. Keep going for ten breaths, in and out. Let the good ideas continue to flow in; they'll still be there for you later.

3 Now you must empty your mind. This is challenging to begin with because thoughts will keep coming back. Use a simple technique of counting slowly to twenty in your head and focus your mind on each number. If an alien thought drifts into your head or tries to muscle in on your focused attention, you will need to start counting from the beginning again. Now, with no thoughts, imagine you are at one with the creative soul of the universe.

4 To begin with, you might not find yourself in this silent place at all. But persevere. Believe you will. Soon you will find the intrusive thoughts go away simply because they can't match the source of untapped potential flowing through you. That's when you are no longer a prisoner to your thoughts and can begin to be creatively engaged in the wealth of the universe.

5 Come out of your meditative state and try to maintain an objective awareness of yourself and how your mind works throughout the day. Also, what happened to those wonderful imagined ideas you let come into your conscious mind as you breathed in? When you remember them, be creative with them. By focusing on one or all of those bright ideas and with objective self-awareness, you will soon have clarity about what it is that you truly seek

PART
TWO

HEALING
WITH
CRYSTALS

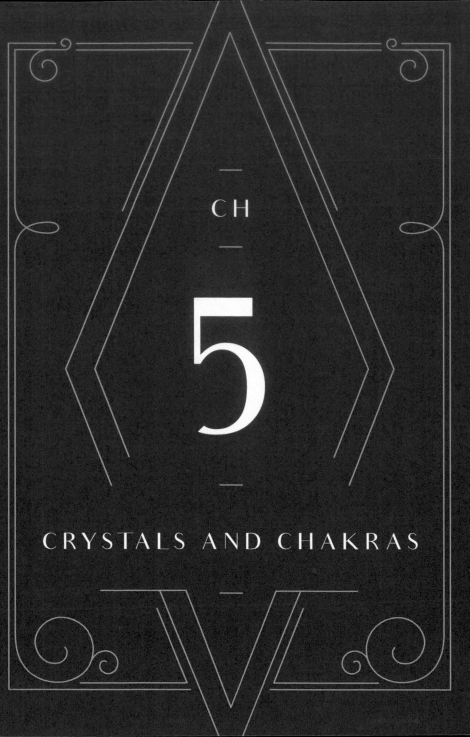

CH

5

CRYSTALS AND CHAKRAS

E astern spiritual traditions maintain that universal energy, known as "prana" in India, and "chi" in Chinese philosophy, flows through the body, linked by seven subtle energy centers known as chakras. The word chakra is a Sanskrit word meaning "wheel."

These energies constantly revolve or spiral around and through our bodies in a vertical direction vibrating at different frequencies. They correspond to the energy of seven colors, which are traditionally associated with seven spiritual gemstones. These stones invoke powerful healing energies and restore the chakra balance.

Crystals respond to the electromagnetic charge that is coursing through our bodies. If our chakra energy is underactive, the vibration of the stones will help to harmonize, balance, and stimulate these energies; similarly, if the energy is overactive, certain stones will help to subdue it. When stones are worn or carried on the body, or placed on the specific chakra centers for healing purposes, they stimulate the corresponding chakra so that both personal spiritual and physical power is restored.

Typically, stones are chosen for each chakra center based on their associated color. By bringing the color frequency of the stone into its corresponding chakra, the energy center is strengthened and balanced. The healing energy emitted by the crystal helps to realign the energy of the chakra, creating harmony in the energy field.

The seven major chakras are vortices of energy that each govern certain aspects of the body, mind, and spirit.

Chakra Center	Color	Location	Body Areas	Qualities	Affirmation
Root	Red	Base of the spine near the pelvis	Bones, small intestine, feet, blood	Strength, vitality, stability, grounding	I am grounded in present-moment consciousness and open to the universal flow.
Sacral	Orange	Between the pubic bone and the navel	Spleen, bladder, ovaries, testes, kidneys	Creativity, sexual energy, emotional balance	I allow the energy of my emotions to flow through me.
Solar Plexus	Yellow	In the hollow area below the sternum in the center of the stomach	Stomach, pancreas, large intestine	Confidence, courage, willpower, mental clarity	I am in touch with my inner power.
Heart	Green and pink	In the center of the chest	Heart, thymus, arms, hands	Balance, love, compassion, harmony	I am heart-centered and feel compassion and love flow through me.
Throat	Light blue	Base of the neck over the throat	Throat, neck, esophagus, thyroid, metabolism	Communication, truth, inner peace, self-expression	I express myself creatively, shining my inner light.
Third Eye	Violet	Between and just above the eyes	Eyes, pineal gland, ears, nose	Intuition, psychic awareness	I am guided by my intuition.
Crown	Red	Top of the head	Brain, pituitary gland, central nervous system	Connection, spirituality, personal transformation, oneness	I am a spiritual being and am one with all that is.

AWAKENING THE CHAKRAS

Crystals are often placed on chakra spots to aid in either reinforcing or subduing the energy, but this is usually done by a skilled practitioner while the subject is lying down. However, you can hold, wear, and carry specific stones for the same purpose.

It's important to know or have a sense of the state of your own chakras. Use the following exercise to help you understand these threshold energies, to increase your awareness of how to open up to their empowering energy, and to close them down when you've finished working with them.

Chakra Awakening

1 Sit on the ground or somewhere comfortable, preferably cross-legged.

2 Start with your root chakra. Move your hands to the base of your spine with your palms facing inwards, without touching your body. Hold your hands about one to two inches away from your lower back. You should feel the energy radiating from this chakra. It may feel warm and solid if it's in good condition; if it's cold or feels floppy, then you may need to empower it by carrying the appropriate crystal.

3 Next, move your hands slowly round to the front of your body and up to the sacral chakra. Hold your hands lightly together with fingers touching in a slight cupping shape, with no gaps. With palms facing your belly, keep your hands still and begin to sense how this chakra feels. Is it watery or does it feel like a gentle flow of energy? (Indicating the fact that it governs the urinary and reproductive system.)

4 Now move your hands up to your solar plexus region, which usually feels warmer and often fiery, governing the pancreas, liver, and nervous system.

5 Move your hands up to the heart chakra, where there is lightness and mobility, governing the thymus gland and circulation. Keep aware of these different areas and your personal reactions to them, not just through your hands but through your sixth sense.

6 Next, move your hands up to the throat chakra and then the third eye chakra. The throat governs communication, the third eye, intuition. What does this feel like in your own words?

7 Finally, at the crown chakra hold your hands above your head and feel the energy buzzing and radiating from the area concerned with your higher or spiritual self.

8 Place your hands back down in your lap. All the chakras have been refreshed and awoken by your awareness of them. Close your eyes and now imagine closing down each chakra as if you were closing a pair of window shutters to guard and save the energy.

REINFORCING STONES

When your chakra energy is weak or not functioning as it should, these crystals will help to stimulate and balance your well-being.

Garnet

Chakra: Root

Red garnets were favored in Greek and Roman antiquity and became known for their power to stimulate business success and career goals. Placing three or more garnets on your desk will help you to achieve your professional aims. When worn as jewelry, garnets aid popularity and self-esteem, and bring a sense of spiritual understanding and empathy to emotional relationships.

Ruby

Chakra: Sacral

The ancient Chinese Taoists considered the ruby to be the stone of fertility and virility. They were laid beneath the foundation of ancient Chinese and East Asian buildings to secure good fortune to the structure. Rubies empower you with financial know-how and make you feel good to be you. The ruby makes you realize that you have an individual purpose and destiny.

Topaz

Chakra: Solar Plexus

Topaz enhances imagination and activates the law of attraction. Topaz is used to invoke faith and belief in one's spiritual quest, and is also a great stone for artists, fashion designers, architects, writers, decorators, or anyone who needs to boost their creativity. The most famous topaz, known as the "Braganza diamond," set in the Portuguese crown jewels, is colorless, and was originally thought to be a diamond.

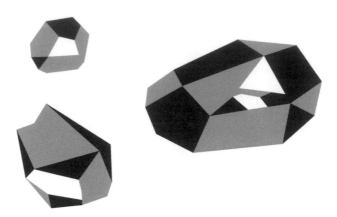

Pink Tourmaline

Chakra: Heart

According to an old Egyptian legend, tourmaline, on its long journey up from the center of the Earth, passed over a rainbow. In doing so, it assumed all the colors of the spectrum, and it is still often called the "gemstone of the rainbow." The name tourmaline comes from the Singhalese words "tura mali" or "stone with mixed colors." Pink tourmaline is the most important for spiritual work and symbolizes compassion, love, warmth, and empathy.

Sapphire

Chakra: Throat

An old myth says that the Ten Commandments given to Moses were written on tablets of sapphire. The sapphire's spiritual powers of communication evoke in the wearer an ability to be enlightened by divine wisdom and, on a more worldly level, to communicate effectively. Empowering the wearer with spiritual enlightenment and inner peace, the sapphire is believed to boost psychic powers such as psychokinesis, telepathy, clairvoyance, and astral projection.

Amethyst

Chakra: Third Eye

The true stone of spiritual healing and enlightenment, the amethyst is often used by mystics, psychics, healers, and religious leaders for its intuitive, transcendent, and spiritually awakening properties. Its calming influence on the mind makes the wearer kind and gentle. It also promotes peace, love, courage, protection against thieves, and happiness.

Diamond

Chakra: Crown

Diamonds are made from the same elements as the stars and galaxies. They help us to connect not only to the cosmos, but to our own true power, strength, and autonomy. A symbol of purity and fidelity, the diamond also brings love and clarity to relationships and creates long-term bonds. Diamonds are also energy amplifiers. So negative thoughts will be even more negative when wearing a diamond!

SUBDUING STONES

When our chakras are out of balance because they are overactive, this often manifests in our behavior toward others. These crystals will subdue and restore balance to your moods.

Tourmaline (Black)

Chakra: Root

Brought to Europe by Dutch traders in the eighteenth century, tourmaline was known as the "ash puller," because it was believed that when laid near burning coals for a long time it had the power to attract and then repel the hot ashes. Black tourmaline gives one a sense of grounding, security, and personal power.

Jade

Chakra: Sacral

Jade talismans and amulets have been worn in the Far East since the fourth century BCE. Jade amulets are still highly popular, and jade statues, jewelry, and carved figures are often given to family, lovers, and friends for protection. Jade calms, invokes new romance, self-love and tolerance, and increases trustworthiness and fidelity.

Amber

Chakra: Solar Plexus

When transparent, this fossilized tree resin often reveals tiny insects trapped inside. Thought to draw all forms of disease from the body, amber lightens the mind, removes negative thoughts, and imbues the body with vitality. It also encourages self-expression, patience, and creativity.

Malachite

Chakra: Heart

Thought by the ancient Egyptians to invoke power and sagacity, malachite was once used to line the inside of the pharaoh's headdress in the hope that he would rule wisely. Malachite is also believed to give us the ability to be true to ourselves in relationship to the world, and yet to stay in balance with it.

Turquoise

Chakra: Throat

The word turquoise comes from the French "pierre turquoise," meaning "Turkish stone." This dates to the early Renaissance when European traders and wealthy Venetian merchants often purchased the stones in Turkish bazaars. Thought to be a talisman of luck, success, ambition, and creativity, the stone protects, purifies, and enables the wearer to see and communicate clearly.

Lapis Lazuli

Chakra: Third Eye

The ancient Egyptians prized this stone, believing the gold flecks were fragments of the stars in the sky, or of the gods themselves. Even the robes of priests or royalty were dyed with lapis (ground down to form an incredible dark blue pigment) to indicate their divine status. Today, lapis is worn to help the wearer to accept the truth, and to bring objectivity and clarity.

Opal

Chakra: Crown

In Greek mythology, opals were believed to be Zeus's tears of joy after the victory over the Titans. The stone is said to center and concentrate the mind, promoting happy dreams, optimism, enthusiasm, and creativity. It is also used to release inhibitions and to inspire love and passion.

THE CHAKRA ENERGIES

We now look at each chakra in turn and how to work out if you need to reinforce its power or subdue it, depending on your psychological traits. Be as honest with yourself as you can be, and then the crystals will work honestly with you.

Root Chakra

The base chakra is located at the base of the spine, centered between the last disc of the spine and the pubic bone to the front. This chakra is concerned with our sense of being grounded. It provides a firm base and sense of security, plus it controls the basic functions of the body. If you have a feeble base chakra, you'll feel spaced out and not in touch with the world, or you may feel threatened by other people and unable to get any project under way.

The base chakra is associated with red, and is energized by wearing or carrying a garnet. This stone will enhance your sense of security, release you from fears and self-doubt, and enable you to trust in yourself and others. If you are too dominating, pushy, and angry at the world, then to subdue this energy, use black tourmaline.

Sacral Chakra

Located approximately a hand's breadth below the navel, the sacral chakra is concerned with your sex drive, creativity, and emotional state. It vibrates to the color orange. If this chakra is underactive, you'll have little confidence in your sexuality and will fear getting close to anyone. You may have problems relating to other people and fear they just want you as a sexual object. You may be emotionally manipulative and have very low self-esteem.

By wearing or carrying ruby, you will enhance your ability to flow with your emotions freely and to reach out to others, both sexually and creatively. If your sacral chakra is overactive, you may have a seductive character, be promiscuous, or demand too much from others. To calm down this overactive chakra, wear or carry jade.

Solar Plexus Chakra

Situated between the navel and the breastbone, the third chakra relates to the color yellow and is the seat of personal power. Rather like having one's own inner sun, it gives us a strong ego, a sense of our personal character, individuality, and willpower. If this chakra isn't shining, then we let others dominate us, feel afraid to express our personal opinion, or worry about what others will think about us. If we have too much of this chakra, we're bossy, careless, egotistic, and too proud for our own good.

To calm this overactive chakra, wear or carry amber. To boost this chakra, wear or carry topaz. This will restore your outgoing nature and give you more self-respect and expressiveness. You will enjoy taking on new challenges and have a strong sense of personal power.

Heart Chakra

Situated behind the breastbone and in front of the spine, the heart chakra vibrates to the colors green and pink, and is the center of warm, loving feelings. This chakra is about true compassion, love, and spirituality. It directs our ability for self-love, as well as to give and to receive love. This is also the chakra connecting body and mind with spirit. When this chakra is low, you may be afraid of revealing your feelings for fear of getting hurt.

Wearing or carrying pink tourmaline or rose quartz will restore your compassion, empathy, and a sense of self-love. When this chakra is overactive you may be always helping everyone else and making sacrifices for loved ones, but never give any love to yourself. To subdue an overactive heart chakra, wear or carry malachite.

Throat Chakra

The throat chakra is, of course, located in the lower end of the throat and is the center for thought, communication, music, speech, and writing. Vibrating to the color blue, when this chakra is out of balance you may feel timid, not say much, resent other people who say anything they like, misunderstand others, or just be unable to express your thoughts. Once balanced by wearing or carrying sapphire or aquamarine, you will be musically or artistically inspired, your communication skills will improve, and anything that you need to say will be said.

If you have an overactive throat chakra, you won't listen to anyone else and will think you know all the answers. You're verbose and angry with everyone around you. To correct and subdue an overactive throat chakra, wear or carry turquoise.

Third Eye Chakra

Located in the center of the brow, the third eye vibrates to the color indigo, or violet, and is concerned with inspiration, imagination, and psychic ability. When this chakra is not balanced you may be blind to the truth, non-assertive, afraid of success, and indecisive. You may not have any psychic sense, nor trust your intuition. To boost this chakra, the gemstone to wear or carry is the amethyst.

The third eye in balance can give you access to your higher self and altered states of consciousness. You feel "in tune" with the universal energy, and everything feels as if it's meant to be. You can see the truth of any matter and understand what people are really thinking or feeling. This will restore your intuitive and psychic nature, as well as give you strong imaginative and visualization powers. If this chakra is overactive, you can't come down to Earth, you live with your head in the clouds and are totally irrational. Wearing lapis lazuli will subdue this chakra.

Crown Chakra

Situated on the top of the head, this is the center for true spirituality and enlightenment. It allows for the inward flow of wisdom and brings the gift of cosmic consciousness. When this chakra is unbalanced there may be a constant sense of frustration, no spark of joy, and a frustrated sense of meaninglessness about everything. Balancing energy in this chakra gives you the ability to open up to the cosmic consciousness and connect to the light of the universe flowing through all things. By wearing a diamond, you can boost the crown chakra and improve your own spiritual beliefs, open up a pathway and connection to other realms, or just aid your own spiritual development.

If this chakra is too active, you may think you're a guru, live in a spiritual haze, constantly talk to friends about your psychic powers, or you may be an idealist and eternal optimist who can't see the wood for the trees. To subdue this chakra, wear or carry opal.

CRYSTAL LAYOUT TO BALANCE THE CHAKRAS

The chakra centers are largely responsible for your energetic well-being and overall sense of health. Keeping these energy centers healthy and balanced is an important part of an effective self-care routine. The following crystal layout will bring overactive or underactive chakra centers back into balance so that your energy body is aligned and able to energetically support your physical health. This layout activates the major chakras and opens the energetic pathways in the body that allow energy to flow regularly.

YOU WILL NEED:

• 7 crystals, 1 of each color shown in the diagram

WHAT TO DO:

1 First you need to choose seven crystals to work with. Traditional crystal chakra-balancing layouts use color correspondences to choose stones appropriate for each chakra center. For example, the color red corresponds to the root chakra. The associated color frequency is a simple way to choose stones for this layout. One exception to this general rule is using pink stones at the area of the heart chakra. This chakra is the point of balance between the higher and lower chakra centers, so to honor that connection green and/or pink stones may be placed here. Green stones are seen as corresponding to masculine energy while pink stones connect more with feminine energy. This creates a sense of balance in masculine and feminine, or yin and yang, energy at the heart center. You may also choose each of your chakra stones intuitively for this layout. If you are confident in your inner guidance and your intuitive skills, choosing your stones in this way can offer a more customized approach to chakra balancing with crystal energy. Simply ask for guidance when choosing each crystal and then make your selection from the group of stones that's available to you.

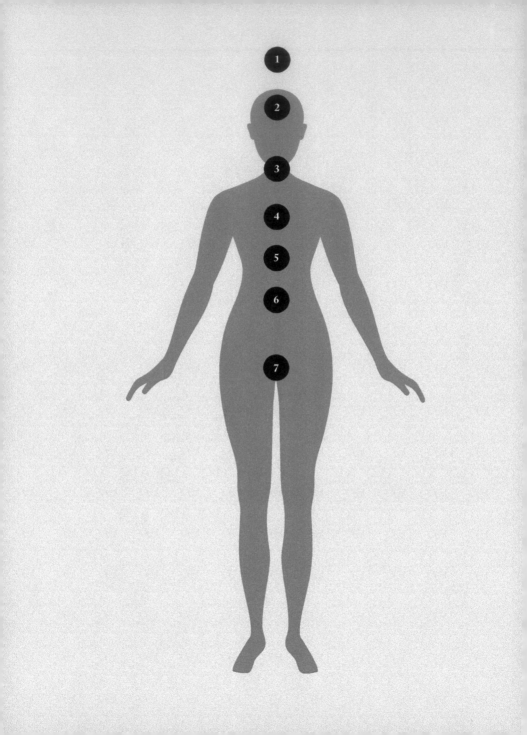

Key

1 Crown chakra crystal (violet)

2 Third eye chakra crystal (indigo)

3 Throat chakra crystal (light blue)

4 Heart chakra crystal (green or pink, see page 99)

5 Solar plexus chakra crystal (yellow)

6 Sacral chakra crystal (orange)

7 Root chakra crystal (red)

2 Begin the chakra-balancing layout by placing a red stone at the area of the root chakra. Next, place the orange stone at the area of the sacral chakra. Continue in this manner, placing the yellow, green (or pink), blue, indigo, and violet crystals over their respective chakras. By placing the stones beginning at the root chakra and working up toward the crown chakra you build the energy of the layout. This allows you to raise your vibration slowly, helping to keep you grounded throughout the session.

3 Remain in the crystal layout for approximately 30 minutes, or until you intuitively feel that your energy centers are aligned and balanced.

4 When you feel ready, remove the purple stone from the crown chakra. Continue in this manner, removing the stones from their respective chakra centers. This will bring the energy back down slowly, keeping you grounded and centered.

CH

6

CRYSTALS FOR
EMOTIONAL HEALING

L ike it or not, your emotions have the capability to influence everything you do. From the way you think about yourself and the world around you to the actions you take and the behaviors you exhibit, you are an emotional creature, ruled by more than logic alone.

Some emotions pass you by without much thought, but other emotional experiences make deep and lasting impressions on you. These are part of the human experience, but rather than allowing them to have a negative impact on your emotional and energetic well-being, you can learn to use crystal energy to cleanse them from your energy field and transmute them into positivity.

The following stones are known for their ability to do just this—heal emotional wounds and trauma and clear emotional debris from your aura. If you have some emotional healing work to do, no matter how big or how small, try working with one or more of the stones in this section.

HEALING YOURSELF

Destress with Amazonite deep breathing exercises.

If you're feeling stressed or anxious, place an amazonite stone over your higher heart chakra, located about halfway between your heart and throat chakras. Take a deep, cleansing breath and slowly exhale. On your next inhalation, feel the soothing amazonite energy enter your body, calming you physically and emotionally. Slowly exhale. Repeat for at least two more breaths, or until you feel at ease.

Attract abundance with Green Apophyllite.

Add a small crystal or cluster to a houseplant to encourage the presence of fairies and nature spirits in your home or sacred space. Green apophyllite is excellent used in the center of a crystal grid for sending distance-healing energy to others. Place a green apophyllite crystal in a place of prominence in your home to attract more abundance into your life. Remember, this is not just financial abundance, but rather an abundance of all that you need to support you. Be sure to sit with this crystal often and make a mental list of all that you would like to draw into your life.

Channel Dioptase in times of despair.

Hold dioptase over your heart chakra in times of despair and ask for the assistance of your guides, angels, or Ascended Masters with what troubles you. Keep the stone with you, in your pocket or purse, to help keep the energy of these helpful beings nearby.

Balance your emotions with Danburite (Pink).

Place a piece of pink danburite over your sacral chakra to balance your emotions, or over your heart chakra to promote self-love, forgiveness, and acceptance. Keep the crystal in place for approximately 10 minutes or until you intuitively feel that the energy has shifted. If the source of your grief or trauma causes you to lie awake at night, unable to sleep, you may place this crystal in your pillowcase or on your bedside table to promote feelings of safety and security.

Rely on Kunzite during big changes in your life.

Keep a piece of kunzite on your person during difficult life periods or major changes (i.e. moving, divorce, career change, retirement, etc.) to help smooth the transition and help you maintain a positive outlook. It is best worn as a pendant over the heart chakra, but may also be carried in your pocket or purse.

Heal deep emotional wounds with Petalite.

To heal deep emotional wounds, hold a piece of petalite in your hands or place one over your heart chakra. Close your eyes and take a deep, cleansing breath. Visualize the stone glowing very bright, like a beacon for your guides and angels. Invite your guides and angels into the space and see them slowly begin to surround you. Think about the emotional aspects of yourself that require deep healing and request that your guides assist you by restoring you to balanced wholeness and a state of perfect emotional well-being. Send your gratitude and love to your guides for their assistance by visualizing the bright light from your petalite moving into the heart center of each of your guides and angels, giving them the gift of sacred crystal energy. Take another deep, cleansing breath and open your eyes.

Release emotional hindrances with Tourmaline (Pink) for personal growth.

Hold a piece of pink tourmaline in your hands for a moment, tuning into its energy. Place it on your desk while you do some writing. Focus your intention on receiving messages from the Akashic Records about your soul's path and any karmic patterning that may be hindering your personal growth or spiritual evolution. Write down everything that comes to you—words, symbols, phrases, sketches of images—anything. Do this without judgement or censorship. When you feel ready, hold the stone in your hands as you review what you have written and try to decipher the messages. Think about what steps you can take going forward to release this negative patterning.

Find tranquility and cleanse your soul with Aquamarine.

Hold a piece of aquamarine in your hands, make yourself comfortable, and close your eyes. Take a deep breath in, inhaling the energy of the stone deep into your body. Let its energy wash over you in a wave of calm. Feel its energy pass through your aura like cleansing ripples of sea water, cleansing your field with the ebb and flow of crystal energy. Focus on the stone in your hands and visualize a blue light begin to pool there. See this light expand outward from your hands, filling your entire body with the gentle energy of the aquamarine stone.

Calm your emotional center with Calcite (Aqua).

Fill a large bowl with water. Make yourself comfortable and drop your aqua calcite stone gently into the center of the bowl. Focus your gaze on the ripples on the water's surface. Allow your eyes to soften, going in and out of focus, and hold your gaze on the ripples. Watch the water as it slowly and gently returns to a calm, still state and feel your inner emotions harmonize with that of the calm water. Remove the stone from the water, dry it gently with a soft cloth and hold it to your heart chakra. Close your eyes and visualize the ripples of your heart, your emotional center, slowing to a calm, still state. Remain in silent meditation for as long as you like, feeling the gentle energy of the aqua calcite stone.

Let Okenite be a symbol for emotional flexibility.

Set this crystal in a place of prominence where you will see it often. Use it as a symbol or reminder to be flexible in your life. It's healthier to be flexible and bend and sway as needed than to be rigid and break or snap against the winds of change. You may even choose to place this stone on your altar or in your sacred space and use it as a point of focus in meditation.

Reduce your anxiety and fear with Lepidolite.
Wear lepidolite as a pair of bracelets (one on each wrist) or earrings to balance the hemispheres of the brain and bring balance and stability to your physical, mental, and emotional bodies. Lepidolite makes the perfect companion for times when you're feeling anxious. Carry a small tumbled stone in your pocket during times of great stress or worry to reduce the discomfort and fear that often accompany anxiety.

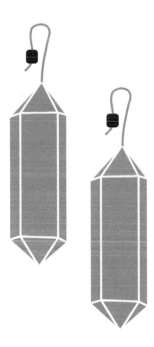

Use Quartz (Celadonite) to protect your inner child.

Place a piece of celadonite quartz in your garden, or on your altar, to attract fairies or nature spirits. You can hold a crystal over your heart chakra to heal your inner child. While holding the stone, intend to release any hurt or trauma from your childhood that may be affecting your patterns of behavior in adulthood. You may even choose to ask for the assistance of fairies and other magical beings to protect and nurture your inner child while this work is carried out.

Release negative energy with Rhodochrosite.

Place this stone in front of you, close your eyes, and drum in rhythm with your heartbeat. Visualize the sound of the drum amplifying the energy of the stone and feel the stone's energy surround you as you drum. Start drumming louder and feel yourself release any negativity or karmic patterning from your being. Slowly reduce the volume of your drumming until it is completely quiet. Take a deep breath in, exhale, and open your eyes.

A CRYSTAL LAYOUT FOR EMOTIONAL WELL-BEING

Keeping the emotional body healthy is an important part of your well-being. The following layout heals emotional wounds, keeps you emotionally balanced, and shields your energy field from negativity.

YOU WILL NEED:
- 7 selenite crystals
- 2 rhodochrosite crystals
- 4 blue lace agate crystals
- 1 cross stone

WHAT TO DO:

1 Place a seven-pointed star of selenite around your body with the point directly above your head. Each of the seven points is representative of one of the layers of the aura. Selenite is a powerful cleansing stone that dissolves energetic imprints that remain within your aura after emotional trauma. Cleansing the energy left by these wounds is the first step toward balancing your emotional body. The seven-pointed star is highly protective and creates an energetic shield that stays with you even after you are no longer within the crystal layout.

2 Next, place a rhodochrosite stone next to each ear in the area of the past-life chakras, just behind the earlobe. These are the centers where information and emotional debris are stored. Rhodochrosite represents acceptance and forgiveness, so these stones will heal and release any residual energy.

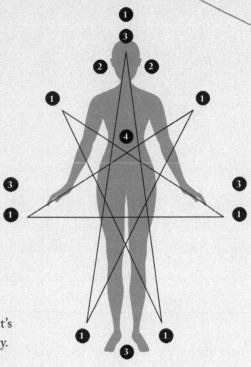

Key

1 Selenite crystal
2 Rhodochrosite crystal
3 Blue lace agate crystal
4 Cross stone

3 After repairing emotional body, it's important to rebalance the energy. Place four blue lace agate stones around your body: one between and just below the feet, one just above the head (between the head and the selenite stone), one on the left side of the body and one on the right side of the body.

4 To enhance the energy of the layout, place a cross stone over the heart chakra. Align the "arms" of the cross with the four blue lace agate crystals surrounding the body. This stone creates an energetic shield around the emotional body, preventing outside energy from entering.

5 Remain within this layout for approximately 15 to 20 minutes or until your emotional body has been healed and balanced.

6 Remove the crystals in the reverse order in which they were placed. Cleanse your crystals thoroughly and re-ground yourself by drinking some water, stomping your feet, or going for a short walk.

HEALING RELATIONSHIPS

Forgive someone with the help of Agate (Blue Lace).
Close your eyes and hold the stone in your hands while focusing on the person requiring your forgiveness. Allow yourself to feel any emotions surrounding the situation, listen to your inner truth about what has happened, and then let go of any unresolved feelings or negativity.

Improve your communication by holding Larimar.
Larimar is best used in a medicine pouch or worn as jewelry. However, you can also hold a larimar stone over your throat chakra to enhance positive communication. Alternatively, try placing a piece of larimar near each of your ears to enhance your ability to hear important messages from totem animals or spirit guides.

Use Pink Mangano Calcite to facilitate a deep connection with others.

Hold the crystal in your receiving hand (usually your nondominant hand—see page 49) and invite the other person to place their receiving hand on top of the stone, so that the crystal is held between each of you. Close your eyes and focus on tuning into the other person's energy field, understanding them physically, emotionally, mentally, and spiritually. Feel yourself connect to the other person so that you're attuned to their energy field and know how best to serve them.

Calm yourself with Eudialyte before engaging in a difficult discussion.

If you know that you must have a difficult discussion with someone, or if a disagreement is imminent, reach for your eudialyte crystal to help you keep a level head. Ask the crystal to help keep you calm and to guide your words and body language to remain cool and collected. Hold the intention to remain emotionally neutral and feel your energy body become balanced by soothing vibrations of the eudialyte stone.

Let Okenite help resolve family and work conflicts.

Place okenite in your kitchen or living room to promote mutual understanding among family members, or in your office or conference room to encourage coworkers to work cooperatively.

Rekindle passion and romance by journaling with Pink Cobalto Calcite.

Place this crystal on a desk or table and take time to sit down and start a journal about yourself and your partner. What do you love most about him or her and about your relationship together? Which aspects of your relationship require healing or forgiveness to move forward? How can you establish trust and vulnerability with one another? What is missing from your relationship that you wish you had? Once you have a list, hold your crystal in your hands and speak these things aloud to manifest them into being for the highest good of you and your partner.

Channel Hiddenite to uncover deceitful people.

To reveal deceitful people, or things that are being hidden from you, hold a hiddenite crystal over your third eye and take mental note of any words, messages, or symbols that come to you intuitively. Take a few moments to jot them down on a piece of paper, and then, while holding your hiddenite crystal in your receiving hand (see page 49), try to decipher the message that is being presented to you.

HEALING THE EARTH

Bring Chrysocolla into nature to heal Earth's wounds.
Go to your favorite spot in nature with your chrysocolla stone. Make yourself comfortable and place the stone on the ground. Hold your hands over the crystal, close your eyes, and tune into the stone's energy. Visualize green, healing light surrounding the chrysocolla. See the light grow and expand out from the stone until it's quite large. Use your hands to push the ball of light toward the Earth's center. Visualize the light traveling through the Earth until it reaches the core. See the light expand, healing the Earth as it passes through every layer, every particle of soil, every plant and animal.

Study with Hiddenite at your side for better retention.
Keep a piece of hiddenite on your desk or table if studying any type of natural or holistic medicine to assist you in fully absorbing the information. Additionally, you can place a piece of hiddenite in your herb garden to promote healthy plant growth.

Use Blue Opal to connect with Gaia.
Place this stone over your heart or third eye while out in nature. Breathe deep and feel your connection to Gaia and all living beings. Know that you are nurtured and supported on your life's journey.

CRYSTAL GRID FOR EMOTIONAL HEALING

This grid can be used to create emotional balance and stability as well as repair emotional wounds. These stones all resonate with the energy of the higher heart chakra, associated with emotional healing, compassion, and forgiveness.

YOU WILL NEED:
- 1 rose quartz crystal
- 6 amazonite crystals
- 6 pink opal crystals
- 1 Seed of Life grid base (pictured)

WHAT TO DO:

1 Begin by gathering your supplies and making sure that all of your crystals have been cleansed. Create an intention statement for your grid such as, "My emotional body is healthy, balanced, and whole." Your intention may be general if you'd just like to focus on overall emotional health, but may also be more specific to your emotional situation when crafting your statement.

2 Set the rose quartz crystal, representing emotional balance, in the center of the Seed of Life shape, as shown in the diagram. Be sure to state your intention, aloud or to yourself, when placing all of your stones.

3 Place the six amazonite crystals, representing compassion and empathy, on the Seed of Life shape, around your central stone. These should be placed in the center of each of the outer circles.

4 Finally, place the six pink opal crystals, representing emotional healing and forgiveness, at the point where two of the outer circles cross, on the outside edge of the shape.

Key

1 Rose quartz crystal

2 Amazonite crystal

3 Pink opal crystal

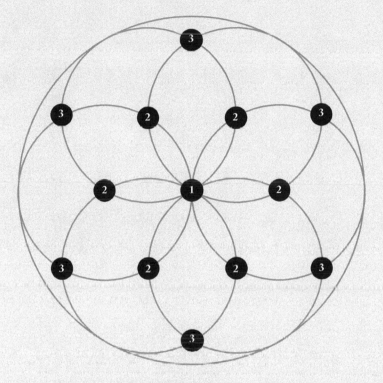

Leave this grid in place for as long as you feel you need the emotional healing energy, but be sure to update your intention statement as needed if your emotional situation changes.

CRYSTALS FOR SPIRITUAL HEALING & DEVELOPMENT

D o you think of yourself as intuitive? Believe it or not, all people have inherent intuitive capabilities, but over time, they lose touch with these natural psychic skills. Rather than accept their intuitive gifts, some people fight against this communication from the spirit.

Crystals can help you to hone your inner guidance in a way that's appropriate for you. They help to boost your confidence in your intuitive abilities as well as create energetic boundaries to keep you safe and protected when opening up psychically.

Additionally, healing crystals can aid in reconnecting with the spiritual aspect of yourself. This enhanced connection can deepen meditation, help you learn to recognize present-moment awareness, and also communicate with your spirit guides and angels. These experiences can help you evolve both personally and spiritually, bringing you closer to your whole, perfect, spiritual self.

HONING YOUR PSYCHE

Use Agate (Shiva's Eye) to awaken your psychic gifts.

Hold the stone in your hands or place it on your third eye chakra. Close your physical eyes and visualize universal energy coming into the stone and moving into your body, filling your body with light. This light keeps you protected while awakening your psychic gifts. Clear your mind of all idle chatter and allow yourself to open up to the messages the universe wishes to send you. They may appear as words, symbols, or pictures, or you may hear them being spoken to you by your guides.

Place Amethyst (Brandberg) in a prominent place to detox your psyche.

Place your Brandberg amethyst crystal in a place of prominence in your home. It is best used on an altar where you can meditate and connect with the Ascended Masters for guidance on your life's journey. You may also hold it in your sending (dominant) hand and pass it through your aura, like a comb, sweeping away any negativity and dissolving psychic debris from your field.

Awaken your inner knowledge with Preseli (Bluestone).

Preseli bluestone is best used in crystal layouts. Placing a stone above the head, at the location of the crown chakra, can activate your inner knowing and connection to the ancients. Alternatively, a stone can be placed over the sacral chakra to promote an inward-looking journey so that you're able to explore the depths of your psyche and your relation to the whole.

Remove psychic debris with Selenite.

Hold a selenite wand in your sending (dominant) hand and pass it through your aura to cleanse negativity from your field. Begin at your head and sweep the energy down toward your feet, removing any psychic debris from your aura.

CRYSTAL GRID FOR INTUITIVE GUIDANCE

This grid can be used to open your third eye chakra and promote intuitive guidance, as well as help you open up the channels of communication with your guides and angels.

YOU WILL NEED:
- 1 azurite crystal
- 8 sodalite crystals
- 2 clear quartz crystal points

WHAT TO DO:

1 Begin by gathering your supplies and making sure that all of your crystals have been cleansed. Create an intention statement for your grid such as, "My third eye chakra is open and I'm willing to receive intuitive guidance." Your intention can be general if you'd just like to focus on overall intuitive guidance, but you may also get as specific as you like to your situation when crafting your statement.

2 Set the azurite crystal, representing intuition and psychic awareness, in the center of your grid area. Be sure to state your intention, aloud or to yourself, when placing all of your stones.

3 Place the eight sodalite crystals, representing connection to your guides and angels, in the shape of an eye, around your central stone, one at each corner of the eye, with three forming the top lid and three forming the bottom lid.

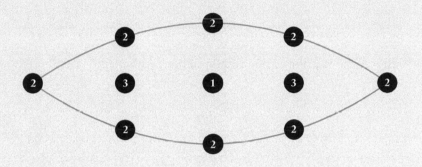

4 Place the two clear quartz points, for amplification of the energy, within
   the eye, on either side of the azurite crystal, pointing from the azurite
   stone toward the corners of the eye. In this way, the energy of the azurite
   expands outward, creating a connection between your intuitive guidance
   and your guides and angels.

Leave this grid in place for as long as you feel you need the intuitive
guidance, but be sure to update your intention statement as required if your
situation changes.

CONNECTING TO SPIRITS

Use Angelite to ask for healing, guidance, and support from angels.
Hold this crystal in your hands or place it on your crystal altar and ask for healing, guidance, and support from your angels and guides. Close your eyes and try to visualize one special angel or guide standing before you, sending pink light into your heart chakra. Feel this pink light balance your emotions and open your heart. Feel your heart connect to all other positive, open hearts on the Earth. Allow yourself to open to this energy and feel vast amounts of love and healing pouring into your heart. Send these same positive, love, and healing energies back out to all of the other hearts to which you're connected. Then, share this pink light with your angel or guide and with your crystal to show your gratitude. When you feel ready, slowly open your eyes.

Use Azurite to connect with guides.

Place this stone on your third eye during meditation or place it on your altar or in your sacred space when you're trying to get in touch with your guides.

Attract nature spirits with Atlantisite.

Atlantisite is an excellent stone to use in your yard or garden. Place a stone in your yard near a favorite plant or tree. Alternatively, apartment dwellers may choose to place the stone in a potted houseplant. The best way to use this stone is to add it to a miniature fairy garden to encourage fairies and nature spirits to visit your space.

Cultivate protective energy with Obsidian (Rainbow Sheen) when channeling guides.

If you're doing any kind of channeling, psychic work, or mediumship, place a piece of rainbow sheen obsidian in a prominent location within your space. Create an affirmation of safety or protective prayer for yourself to keep you shielded during your work. This may be something as simple as, "I am shielded, protected, and secure," to something very specific about the type of psychic work that you do. Hold your hands over the obsidian stone while speaking your affirmation aloud, activating the crystal and filling your space with protective energy.

Find clarity and wisdom from spirit guides with Quartz (Ajoite).

Hold an ajoite quartz crystal up to your third eye chakra and close your eyes. Begin your meditation and picture yourself in a beautiful crystal cave. Start exploring the cave, which is filled with tons of glittering ajoite quartz crystals. Move through the various passages in the cave until you discover a cavern where your spirit guides are waiting for you. Greet them and ask for their wisdom and guidance about any life issues that you'd like clarity about. Allow yourself to receive any messages from your guides. These may come as spoken words, images, pictures, symbols, or feelings. When you're ready, thank your guides, open your eyes, and return to your everyday awareness.

Connect to spirits by communicating through Ametrine.

Write down the name of a specific person or guide that you would like to connect with on a small piece of paper and place the stone atop the paper. Hold your hands over the stone and feel the connection take place between yourself and the spirit, then communicate what you need to say, or listen to messages being shared with you.

CENTERING YOURSELF

Recenter your energy with Auralite-23.

Hold an auralite-23 crystal in your hands and visualize it glowing with bright, fiery, violet light. See this light expand into your space, dissolving any negative energy from within your aura or your environment. Feel your body return to a state of balance and wholeness, easing into the flow of the universe.

Refocus your energy with Celestite on a full or new moon.

Celestite is best used in meditation, but it will also work well just by being placed in your sacred space or on your altar. Alternatively, you may take your celestite outside at night (in a safe place), on the evening of a full or new moon. Hold your celestite crystal up to the moon to charge it with energy. Full moonlight aids manifesting and promotes abundance while new moonlight may help you to break bad habits or start new projects.

Rebalance your chakra centers with Kyanite (Blue).

To balance and harmonize your chakra centers, hold a piece of blue kyanite parallel to your spine over your root chakra for approximately one to two minutes. Next, move the stone to your sacral chakra and hold it in place for an additional one to two minutes. Continue in this manner, moving up through the chakra centers: solar plexus chakra, heart chakra, throat chakra, third-eye chakra, and crown chakra. Once you are finished, take a deep, cleansing breath and stomp your feet to re-ground yourself. Cleanse your stone thoroughly.

Balance a room with Shattuckite to promote a connection to the universe.

Shattuckite can create a positive shift in energy if placed in the center of a room. Put a shattuckite stone on your altar or in your sacred space to create feelings of harmony and tranquility in the room, so that you can recharge your personal power when you're in the space. When used in this way, your shattuckite stone acts as a point of connection to the universe and promotes spiritual growth and ascension.

Further spiritual development with Moldavite.

Holding moldavite during meditation is the best way to use this crystal for spiritual development.

Use Moonstone (Black) to reconnect with lunar energy.

To truly bond with the energy of this crystal, use it during every major moon phase for one full lunar cycle (new, waxing crescent, first quarter, waxing gibbous, full, waning gibbous, third quarter, waning crescent, back to new). Set aside 5 to 10 minutes every evening during each phase of the moon cycle to sit and meditate with your crystal, feeling yourself become connected to the lunar energy.

Let Scolecite identify the obstacles in your life preventing spiritual growth.

Lie down somewhere you will be comfortable and can remain undisturbed for a length of time. Place the scolecite above your head at the area of your crown chakra. Take a deep breath in, close your eyes, and ask the spirit of the stone to reveal to you what needs to be cleansed and transformed in this lifetime in order to move forward on your spiritual journey. Allow yourself to dive deeply into the energy of your crystal, remaining in this position for about an hour. Be mindful of any messages or feelings that come through during the experience. When you feel ready, open your eyes, remove the stone, cleanse it thoroughly, and record your experience in your crystal journal.

Enhance manifestation with Quartz (Spirit).

A spirit quartz cluster is excellent used in the center of a crystal grid for manifesting. You may place a small written affirmation beneath the stone to enhance its effects.

Let Moonstone (Rainbow) help you manifest your desires.

Place this crystal outside, overnight, to charge it with lunar energy on the night of a full moon. Then write down what you'd like to manifest on a small piece of paper and place the charged crystal atop the paper to call your desire into being.

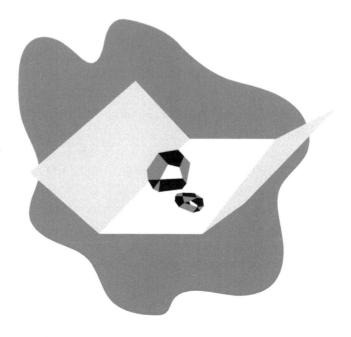

Embark on a personal spiritual retreat with Nuummite.

Schedule a mini spiritual retreat for yourself for an entire day. Plan your whole day, from what you will eat (and having all of your meals prepared in advance), to how you will spend your time. It's important that you make an effort to disconnect from the outside world on this day and focus on inner work. A large portion of your day should be dedicated to meditating in a dark, quiet room, free from distractions. Create a sacred space for yourself where you can connect with the energy of your nuummite stone. Make yourself comfortable and place the crystal on your third eye chakra, allowing yourself to open fully to the experience of the crystal's energy during your meditation.

Charge Jadeite (Blue) with moon energy to call blessings into your life.

Jadeite works to carry blessings and amplify them for manifesting. Take your crystal outside (in a safe place) on the night of a full moon, which resonates with manifestation. Hold it in your hands, above your head, and up to the moonlight to be charged with the full moon energy. Ask for the blessings of the universe to aid in your manifesting efforts. Carry your charged stone with you to call these blessings into your life

A CRYSTAL LAYOUT FOR INTUITIVE GUIDANCE

Crystals can work wonders in helping open you to receiving intuitive guidance and messages from your spirit guides and angels. These messages are important because they act like signposts, guiding you to follow your soul path throughout your life's journey. The crystals in this layout can open your third eye chakra and help to facilitate a connection with divine energy. These stones also assist you in tapping into your psychic gifts so that you learn to trust your own inner guidance and use it to make decisions and grow, both as a person and a spiritual being.

YOU WILL NEED:
- 1 amethyst crystal
- 1 Herkimer diamond quartz crystal
- 1 angelite crystal

WHAT TO DO:

1 Begin this layout by placing an amethyst crystal over your third eye chakra, between and just above your two physical eyes. Amethysts work to open you to your inner guidance if you've been closed off to it, as well as help you begin to trust these important messages as they come through. If your intuition is that of a child lost in the woods, then amethysts are the breadcrumbs that help lead you back home and awaken to your soul's calling.

Key

1 Amethyst crystal

2 Herkimer diamond quartz crystal

3 Angelite crystal

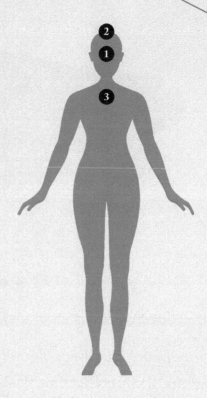

2 Next, place a Herkimer diamond quartz above the amethyst, near your hairline, so that the terminations of the crystal are parallel with the spine. By aligning the points of the crystal in this way, you clear away any blockages within your chakra system that may be impeding your intuitive development. A Herkimer diamond is a powerful cleanser of energy, clearing your energetic pathways so that your intuitive messages can come through loud and clear, connecting you with your guides and angels.

3 Finally, place an angelite stone on your throat chakra. This will help to facilitate communication with your spirit guides and angels. After placing this stone, you can invite your guides or angels into the space to share their wisdom and knowledge with you. If you have a specific question, you may ask it once you feel the presence of your guides in the space.

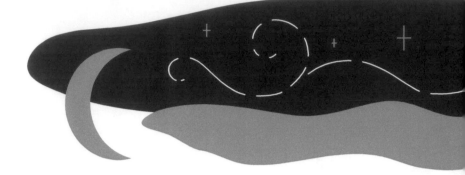

DREAM WORK

Use Amethyst to reconnect with your spiritual side or promote sweet dreams.

Wear amethyst as a ring or pendant to help you reconnect with your spiritual side. You can also tuck a small, tumbled stone into your pillowcase to promote sweet dreams, or place a crystal on your bedside table to help with dream recall and interpretation.

Practice lucid dreaming with Amethyst (Chevron).

A few minutes before bed, hold your crystal while focusing on the issue you'd like to resolve through dream-healing work. If you do not have a specific issue that needs resolving, or if you'd just prefer to explore the dream state, then you can intend to become aware that you're dreaming from within the dream state so that you're able to explore as you wish. Speak your intention aloud or to yourself and tuck the stone into your pillowcase. Picture the stone in your mind's eye as you drift off to sleep with the intention to see the stone from within your dream state, as a visual cue that you're dreaming so that you can take conscious control of your dream.

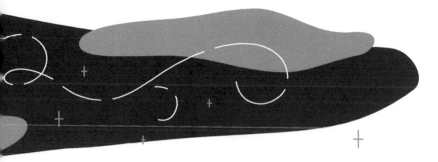

Let Quartz (Dream) help you achieve a dream state.

Place a dream quartz cluster on your bedside table and look at it before falling asleep. When you close your eyes, try to picture it in your mind's eye. Set an intention for your dream state—lucid dreaming, dream healing, or intuitive dreaming. Try to have the crystal be the very last thing you think about before you fall asleep. When you awake, hold your crystal and reflect on your dreams. Write down a few messages in your dream journal (if you have one) or on a piece of paper, about your intention for the night before and whether or not you were able to achieve your dreaming goals.

Set dream intentions with Cavansite.

Place cavansite on your bedside table. Before going to sleep, set an intention for your dream state. Your intention may be spiritual exploration, astral travel, dream healing, or even connection with your guides. As you drift off to sleep, hold this intention clearly in your mind and feel yourself surrounded by the energy of the cavansite stone. When you awake, record your experiences in your dream journal or crystal journal, if you have one, and try to interpret any messages that you received. If the meaning does not come to you right away, hold your cavansite stone in your hands and ask for clarity in regard to the interpretation. This can be a powerful way to receive messages and wisdom from your guides about important life decisions and your spiritual growth.

FOR MEDITATION AND MANIFESTATION

Refresh your mind with Quartz (Shamanic Dream) through meditation.

Find a quiet place to meditate where you won't be disturbed. Hold a shamanic dream quartz crystal in your hands and gaze into its depths. Allow your conscious mind to slowly give way to your subconscious (your inner self) as you explore the depths of the crystal's inner landscape. Take note of the beauty of the crystal's interior; appreciate how the minerals flow and swirl together, in natural perfection. Let all thoughts slip away from you and lose yourself for a time in the peace of the crystal. Once you have achieved a sense of mindfulness, close your eyes and tune into your own energy. When you feel ready, you may open your eyes and return to the present moment.

Receive guidance with Covellite.

Make yourself comfortable in a place where you won't be disturbed. Dim the lights so that you can soften your gaze and relax your eyes. You may want to light a candle or have a small light source nearby. Hold your covellite stone in your hands and think about an area of your life for which you require some guidance. Begin to look at the stone's surface. Notice its sheen and shimmer. Allow your eyes to go in and out of focus and stare at your crystal. Attempt to see any images or symbols in the play of light on the stone's surface. Once you do, try to interpret the meanings of these symbols as they relate to your question.

Practice personal meditation and journaling with Aqua Aura Quartz.

Aqua aura quartz is probably best used as a personal meditation stone. To deepen your connection with your crystal, try meditating with it at least three times per week for one month. Before each meditation session, be sure to set an intention or goal for yourself and what you'd like to achieve (whether it be stillness of mind, connecting with guides, self-awareness, or something else). Keep a meditation journal during this time and take note of any interesting or seemingly significant experiences that you have with your stone.

Amplify your meditation with Apophyllite.

Hold the stone in your hands for a high-frequency crystal meditation. You may also try placing a piece of apophyllite on your altar or in your sacred space to send healing energy to those at a distance. Alternatively, you can place a natural apophyllite pyramid in the center of a crystal grid for an extra burst of energy and amplification of your intention.

Use Jadeite (Lavender)to help develop a regular meditation routine.

It can be difficult to meditate regularly, but lavender jadeite provides gentle encouragement. Make a meditation ritual for yourself that somehow incorporates your crystal. Try setting it in a place where you will see it often and use it as a reminder to make time for mindfulness. Or, commit to a five-minute meditation each day for five days. Hold your lavender jadeite at the start of each meditation to help keep you motivated. At the end of the five days, take two days off, and then start up your five-day schedule again. Take time to connect with your lavender jadeite during your two days off to keep you on the right track with your routine.

Access crystal wisdom with Quartz (Tibetan) through deep meditation.

To facilitate deep meditation and to access the wisdom and knowledge stored in these crystals, place one on your third eye chakra. Take a deep breath in, close your eyes, and feel the energy of the stone begin to gentle pulse on your forehead. Chant the mantra, "Om," and feel the energy of the crystal expand, entering your third eye. Feel the energy continue to grow until it fills your entire body. Remain in silent meditation with your crystal for as long as you like.

LIFE CHANGES AND DECISIONS

Use Barite (Blue) to help with difficult decisions.
When you have a difficult choice to make, hold this crystal in your hands and think of all of the potential outcomes of making your decision. Ask the crystal to show you any additional options that you may not be aware of. Sit in quiet meditation with the stone, allowing any possible scenarios to enter your mind. Take time to tune into the stone's energy and request that it help you make the decision that is for your highest good. After your meditation, thank the crystal for its assistance and cleanse it thoroughly.

Use Iolite to help choose between two paths.

If you feel as though you're at a fork in the road, write down the different options available to you, each on a separate piece of paper. Hold an iolite crystal above each piece of paper, one at a time, and determine which seems to make the stone shine brightest. This is likely the best decision for you at this time, but listen to your inner guidance as the iolite may be calling your attention to that option for other reasons.

Use Purpurite to channel your inner phoenix during big life changes.

When you're undergoing big changes in your life, keep a purpurite stone with you in your pocket or purse so that its energy remains in your field, supporting you during the transformation. You may also want to sit quietly, holding your purpurite stone, and visualize a mighty phoenix in your mind's eye. See this phoenix surrounded by violet light emanating from your stone. Then, visualize the phoenix growing smaller and smaller and flying into the interior of your stone, residing there to help you through these life changes, acting as a symbol of your personal growth.

PRACTICE SELF-CARE

Ask for healing energy from the Earth with Silica (Quantum Quattro).

Take a piece of quantum quattro silica out into your favorite place in nature. Also bring along a bell or chime and a piece of fruit. Sit down and place your quantum quattro stone on the ground in front of you. Ring your bell or chime to call on nature spirits in the area and ask them to surround you and support you during this Earth healing ceremony. Hover your hands over the stone and visualize it glowing with bright light. See this light expand and move deep down into the Earth, all the way to the Earth's core. Hold the intention to offer the Earth this healing energy. Then, offer the piece of fruit to the Earth spirits to show your gratitude for their support during the process.

Acknowledge your achievements by wearing a Sapphire (Blue).
Wear a piece of blue sapphire jewelry to help recognize your achievements
and celebrate them.

Refocus your mind on the present with Fluorite (Lavender).
If you're beginning a new spiritual practice, or studying something new,
keep lavender fluorite near you. Having the stone in view is a great visual
reminder to check in with yourself and be sure you're present. If you start to
lose your train of thought or you find your mind beginning to wander, reach
out and hold your stone. Take a few deep breaths and remind yourself to
focus on the present moment. Feel the crystal's energy help to center you
and then return to your task when you're ready.

Tether yourself to the Earth with Prasiolite.
Place a tumbled prasiolite stone on the floor any time you're feeling
ungrounded or "spacey." Gently place the soul of your foot into the stone
(just enough to make contact, but without applying pressure or creating any
sense of discomfort). Keep your foot in this position for about 30 seconds
and then repeat the process with your other foot.

Enhance a healing session with Quartz (Angel Aura).
To enhance the effectiveness of a healing session, place an angel aura quartz
cluster on your altar, in your healing space, or beneath the massage table.

Release trauma with Charoite by finding its origin.

Place this stone on your third eye chakra and think about patterns or trauma that you'd like to release. Attempt to recall any past lives where this energy may have been imprinted upon your spiritual body. You do not have to relive the negative experience, but rather just simply discover the lifetime where it occurred in order to reassure yourself that it has no practical bearing on your current lifetime. Take a deep breath in, and forcefully exhale while intending to release the energy out of your third eye chakra. Thoroughly cleanse your crystal.

Make a wish with Seraphinite.

Hold a piece of seraphinite in your hands and call on your guardian angels and spirit guides. Make a wish or ask for assistance in manifesting something you desire. Place the stone on your altar or in your sacred space. Make time to sit with your crystal each day, for just two or three minutes, to reaffirm your request, until your wish has been granted.

Undergo soul searching with Tanzanite (Blue).

Tanzanite is best used as a piece of jewelry worn during times of transformation and soul searching.

Realign your body with Opal (Boulder).

Hold a piece of boulder opal in your sending (dominant) hand and pass it over your chakra centers, beginning at your root chakra and moving up the spine toward your crown chakra to realign them and bring you an overall sense of wellness and balance.

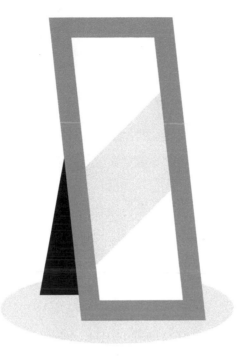

Enhance physical self-esteem with Quartz (Golden Rutilated).
To enhance your self-confidence and create positive thoughts about your body image, stand in front of the mirror while holding your golden rutilated quartz. Every day for one week, speak aloud one thing that you find beautiful or likeable about yourself while holding your crystal and gazing at your reflection. The following week, you should speak two positive traits while holding your crystal. Continue in this manner, adding one new thing each week until you feel confident, beautiful, loved, and lovable.

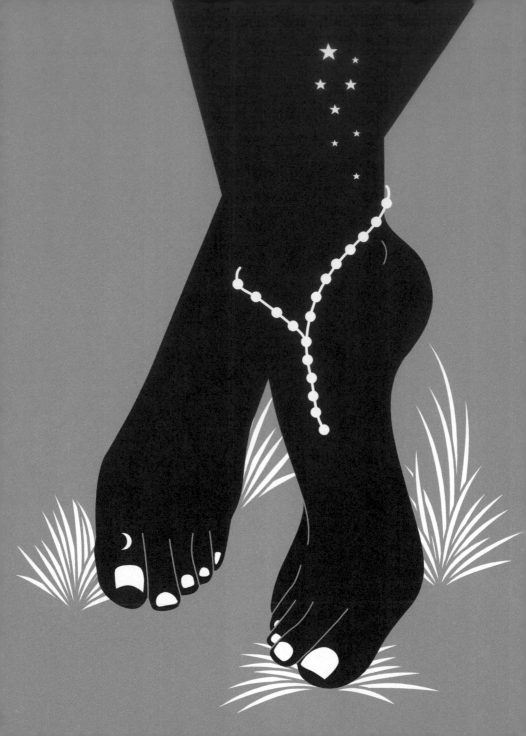

Replace your anxieties with self-love using Anhydrite (Blue).

Lie down and make yourself comfortable, place two pieces of blue anhydrite, one over each shoulder, as if they were angel's wings. Close your eyes and feel yourself become lighter, releasing any worry or anxiety that may be weighing you down. Focus on the area of your solar plexus chakra and feel yourself filled with self-love and self-worth. Alternatively, you can place a single stone directly over your solar plexus chakra, aligned so that it is parallel with your spine. Visualize golden light being drawn from the universe into the stone where it pools at the area of your solar plexus.

Wear Lapis Lazuli to harness your inner strength.

For thousands of years, people have been donning lapis jewelry to harness inner strength. It is still a beneficial practice today.

Live in the moment with Danburite.

Take your danburite crystal outside on a sunny day. Find a grassy area, a beach, or someplace Earthy and take off your shoes so that your bare feet can connect with the Earth's energy. Hold your crystal up to the sun and see it filled with light. Feel the crystal store up this vibrant energy and pull your danburite close to your heart. Hold it there, feeling yourself become fully present in this moment, feeling happiness and peace.

REMOVING NEGATIVITY AND STRESS

Draw on Labradorite to ward off negativity.

Carry labradorite with you or wear it as jewelry for constant protection from negativity.

Use Vesuvianite (Purple) to recall happy memories.

When you're feeling sad or blue, reach out for your purple vesuvianite crystal. Hold it in your hands and try to recall as many happy memories as you can. These can be small memories or reflections on big life events. Hold your focus on the way you feel when reflecting on these memories and allow that feeling to fill you up energetically. Practice this exercise at least once a week as a routine self-care practice, or do it daily during times when you feel you need the extra energy boost.

Transform negative into positive energy with the help of Euclase.

Hold a euclase crystal up to your third eye chakra. Take a deep breath in and close your eyes. Visualize pulling blue energy in through the euclase, and into your third eye chakra. Feel the light blue energy of this stone begin to gently dissolve away any mineral deposits from your pineal gland. Take another deep breath in, and as you exhale, release any remaining negativity out of your body. See this negativity being transformed into positive energy as it is sent out into the universe. Intend that only the energy which is for your highest good will remain within your body. Open your eyes and cleanse your stone thoroughly.

Organize your thoughts and tasks with Hypersthene to destress.
Hold your hypersthene stone in your hands when you're feeling
overwhelmed by your day-to-day responsibilities and tasks. Close your eyes
and think about all of the things on your "to-do" list. When you have a
good mental list, place your stone near you and write down all of the things
you'd like to get accomplished. Highlight the things that are urgent and
important and prioritize them into an action plan. Hold your stone for a
few minutes to energize yourself and then get started with your list.

HEALING GROUPS OF PEOPLE

Foster tranquility with Jadeite (Blue).

If you're lucky enough to obtain several pieces of blue jadeite, you can use it to create a tranquil space by placing one stone in each corner of a room.

Enhance group harmony with Quartz (Faden).

To bring harmony among the members of a group, place a faden quartz in the center of the meeting space. Ask that all group members join hands, close their eyes, and tune into the energy of the stone. Have each member in the group speak aloud a positive intention for the group meeting for the day. Feel the energy of the faden quartz embrace everyone in the space.

Increase group cooperation with Hemimorphite (Blue).

To enhance group cooperation, place a piece of blue hemimorphite in the center of your meeting space. If you need better harmony at home, try placing this stone in the room your family spends the most time in (likely the living room or kitchen). If cooperation is necessary at work, placing the stone in a conference room or office area may be useful. You can also bring the crystal with you to meetings or get-togethers and keep it discretely tucked away in your pocket or purse.

Use Sugilite to erase negative energy at your workplace.

To clear negative energy in your work environment, place a small sugilite stone in each corner of the space. If something more discreet is necessary, you may want to create a sugilite spray to mist the space, subtly introducing the vibrational frequency of the stone. Place a tumbled sugilite crystal in a small, glass bowl filled with distilled water and leave it to soak overnight. Remove the crystal and pour the water into a small spray bottle. Mist your work area with the sugilite water to promote harmony and group cooperation.

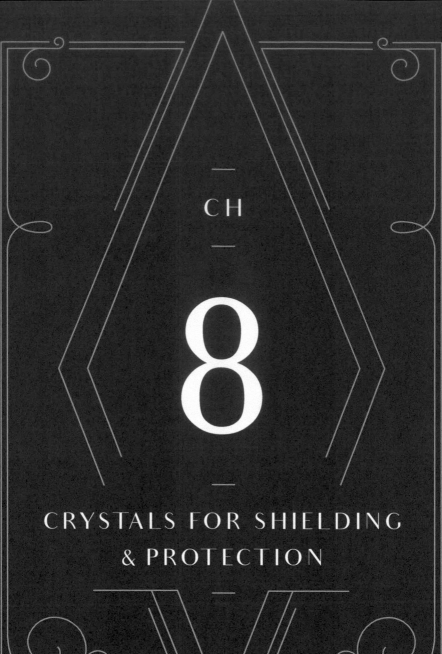

CH

8

CRYSTALS FOR SHIELDING
& PROTECTION

Y our energy body is in a constant state of flux. In addition to being ever-evolving, it is also highly sensitive to the influence of outside energy. Your energy field is part of what helps give you your sixth sense and understand the world around you. However, if you don't take steps to create healthy energetic boundaries, you can become completely bombarded by this outside energy. This lack of shielding and protection can leave you feeling depleted, lethargic, and completely drained. In this section, you'll learn about crystals that can help prevent this from happening, as well as some simple ways to start using them to shield and protect your energy body.

Some crystals can even help to support you energetically to keep your aura clear from outside influence and emotionally charged energy. This keeps you happier and healthier by ensuring that you stay feeling fresh and rejuvenated because you're not depleted. This is especially important to lightworkers, empaths, and psychics who regularly connect with other beings and energy in the environment.

CREATING A PROTECTIVE SPACE/SHIELD

Wear Avalonite as a shield.

This stone is best used when worn as jewelry over your heart chakra or when held in your dominant hand, as if it were a shield. It can also be held over the third eye chakra during meditation to call upon the strength and wisdom from the legendary figures of Avalon and Camelot.

Create a sacred space with Aventurine (White).

Use several pieces of white aventurine, one in each corner of a room, to create a sacred space for your spiritual practice. After placing the stones, stand in the center of the room and visualize the crystals connected by lines of energy, linking them together so that they act in harmony. Use this space for meditation, yoga, or religious ceremony to deepen your spiritual work and keep you motivated to keep up on your practice.

Create a shield of protective energy with Bytownite.

Hold a bytownite stone over your solar plexus chakra and take a deep breath. Feel the energy of the crystal dissolving any psychic debris, negative karma, or unwanted energy from your physical body. Gently exhale. One your next inhalation, feel the stone's energy extend into your aura and chakra centers, removing any ties to soul contracts that will not serve your purpose for this lifetime. Feel all cords and attachments being dissolved. As you exhale, breathe out any remaining negativity. Feel the energy filling your physical and energetic bodies with golden light, creating a shield of protective energy around you. Breathe in again, this time feeling yourself become empowered on a physical, emotional, and spiritual level. Hold this energy in your being for a count of three. Exhale gently. Cleanse the stone thoroughly.

Wear Heliodor as a pendant for protection.

Heliodor is best used by wearing it as a pendant on a long chain so that it hangs over the area of the solar plexus chakra.

Use Larvikite to amplify protection or create a protective grid.

Larvikite is useful when added to a protective medicine pouch. It can also be used to create a simple protective grid by placing a stone in each corner of a room. When creating this larvikite grid, you should set an intention that the stone's energy help to support and protect you. You may keep this intention general, but it's best to be as specific as possible in relation to your unique situation.

A CRYSTAL LAYOUT FOR SHIELDING AND PROTECTION

Keeping yourself protected is an important part of your energy-healing practice. The following layout helps to shield your auric body from the negative energy of others or your environment. When you work preventatively to stay protected, you keep yourself from being depleted of the energy that works to keep you healthy and balanced.

YOU WILL NEED:

- 8 smoky crystals
- 1 tektite crystal
- 1 hematite crystal
- 2 labradorite crystals

WHAT TO DO:

1 Begin this layout by placing a vertical line of four smoky crystals on either side of your body, a total of eight stones. Be sure that the crystals are in alignment within each line and that the two lines are parallel to one another. The vertical lines of crystals should be approximately the same distance away from the body. For example, if the line of crystals on the left side of the body is approximately a foot away from the left arm, then the line of crystals on the right side of the body should be about a foot away from the right arm. These crystals will dissolve any negative energy or psychic debris that has accumulated in your field. They also prevent new energy that's not for your highest good from entering your aura, filtering out negativity and allowing only positive energy to pass through the barrier they create.

2 Next, place a tektite stone above the head in the area of the crown chakra. The energy of tektite creates a psychic shield around your physical body and your aura.

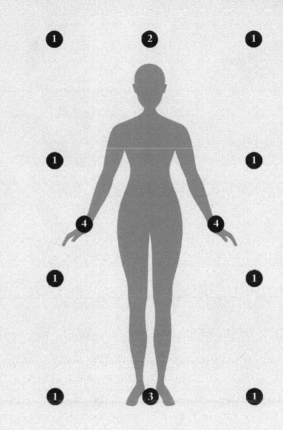

Key
1 Smoky crystal
2 Tektite crystal
3 Hematite crystal
4 Labradorite crystal

3 Now place a piece of hematite between and just below the feet. This will help keep you grounded and connected to the energy of the earth. When you're rooted into the earth, you can continuously pull in a constant stream of energy into your body to keep your reserves full so that you do not become depleted.

4 In each of your hands, hold a piece of labradorite to shield your physical and energetic bodies from picking up on outside energy.

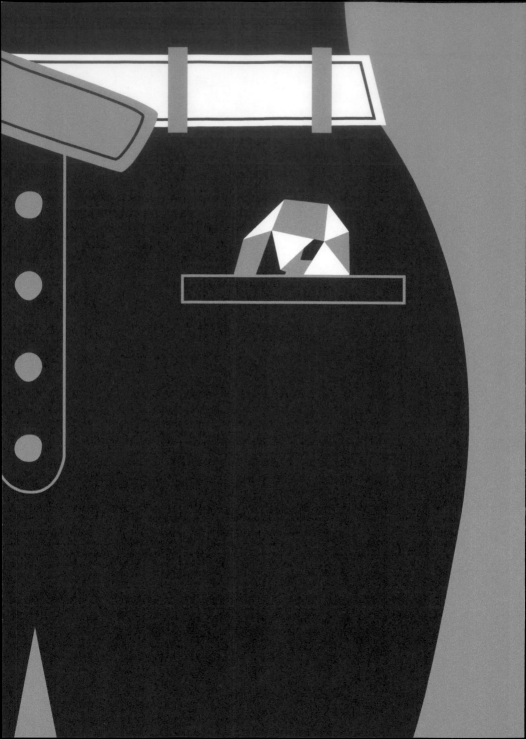

WEARING CRYSTALS FOR PROTECTION

Carry Calcite (Golden) with you every day for protection.

Golden calcite works most effectively as a protective stone if it is carried with you continuously. Keeping the stone in your pocket, or having it specially wire-wrapped into a crystal pendant would be a simple way to keep its energetic vibration in your auric field at all times. To amp up the energy and effects of your stone, you may choose to create a protective prayer, or confidence-boosting affirmation, and speak it aloud each time you use the crystal.

Carry Cross Stone on your receiving side for protection.

Keep a piece of cross stone in a pocket on the receiving side of your body (see page 49) to fully absorb this stone's protective qualities.

Wear Diopside (Black Star) to protect you while channeling.

Wearing a black star diopside pendant will help to keep you safe and protected during channeling or other intuitive work. Alternatively, using a black star diopside stone in the center of a crystal grid can really amplify your manifesting efforts.

Counteract negative people with Pietersite.

If you know you're going to be somewhere with negative people or negative energy in the environment, slip a piece of pietersite into your pocket. Your crystal will shield you, like a cloak of invisibility, from difficult people and situations. Pietersite sends positive vibrations into the space, counteracting the negativity of others so that you don't feel overwhelmed by their energy.

MAINTAINING YOUR AURA

Reduce anxiety with Kyanite (Black).

If you're feeling anxious or stressed, hold black kyanite in your sending (dominant) hand and use it to sweep through your aura. Stress and worry come from an excess of energy in your physical, mental, and emotional bodies, so by using black kyanite to remove the energetic debris, you can clear your energy field and calm your physical body. Begin at the top of your head, and holding the kyanite like a comb, sweep any negativity down toward the Earth. Cleanse your crystal thoroughly when you're finished.

Use Garnet (Spessartine) in the morning to protect your auric field.

If you're an empath or find that you're just sensitive to the energy of others, try 5 to 10 minutes each day to hold your spessartine garnet as soon as you wake up. Focus on breathing in the energy of the stone and visualize it filling your aura. This will allow the energy of the stone to create a protective shield around your auric field so that you remain protected throughout your day.

Minimize your negativity with Halite (Blue).

Hold a piece of blue halite in your sending (dominant) hand and pass it through your aura making small, counterclockwise circles. This helps to draw negativity from your field and dissolve any cords or connections that may be infringing upon your energy. Alternatively, you can place the stone in your sacred space to keep it clear of negativity.

Meditate with Shiva Lingam for protection.

Place your Shiva lingam stone in a place of prominence within your sacred space and meditate with it often.

Look into Ulexite to see through deception.

Gather together a ulexite stone, a pen or pencil, and some scraps of paper. Make yourself comfortable in your sacred space and ponder a situation where you suspect someone is being intentionally deceitful. Write down the names of each person involved in the situation, each on a separate scrap of paper. Hold the ulexite over each person's name and attempt to read the names through the ulexite stone. Those that come through very clearly are being honest and transparent with you, while those whose names appear dull or cloudy are most likely hiding something of importance.

CRYSTAL GRID FOR SHIELDING AND PROTECTION

This grid can be used to create an environment where you will be protected from outside energy as well as creating an energetic shield around you so that you'll be protected when leaving the space.

YOU WILL NEED:
- 1 black tourmaline crystal
- 6 peridot crystals
- 6 labradorite crystals
- 1 Seed of Life grid base (pictured)

WHAT TO DO:

1 Begin by gathering your supplies and making sure that all of your crystals have been cleansed. Create an intention statement for your grid such as, "I am safe and protected. I am shielded from negative influences both physical and energetic." Your intention may be general if you'd just like to focus on overall protection but may also be as specific as you like to your situation when crafting your statement.

2 Set the black tourmaline crystal, representing intense protection, in the center of the seed of life shape. Be sure to state your intention, aloud or to yourself, when placing all of your stones.

3 Place the six peridot crystals, known for disintegrating and dissolving negative energy from your aura, on the Seed of Life shape, around your central stone. These should be placed in the center of each of the outer circles.

4 Finally, place the six labradorite crystals, used for shielding, at the point where two of the outer circles cross, on the outside edge of the shape.

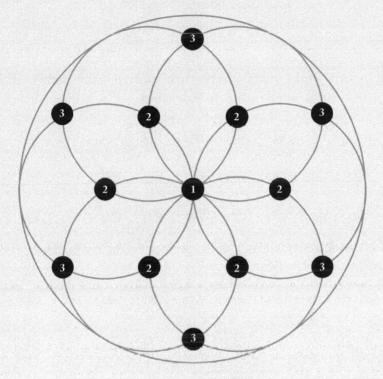

Leave this grid in place for as long as you feel you need the protective energy, but be sure to update your intention statement as needed if your situation changes.

CONNECTING WITH YOURSELF AND OTHERS

Strengthen your intuition with Jasper (Orbicular).

Hold this stone while meditating near any body of water to tune in to the energy of the water element and to strengthen your intuition.

Use Halite (Pink) to spiritually connect with your partner.

Place a pink halite in your bedroom or somewhere you spend a great deal of time with your partner. If your partner is open to working with crystals try performing the following technique together. Both you and your partner should sit together on your floor or your bed with the crystal placed between you. Hold hands with your partner, your right hand in their left, and your left hand in their right, above the crystal. You should both close your eyes and tune in to one another's energetic frequency. Hold the intention of ultimate compassion and understanding while you work to connect to the other person. Stay in this state for about five minutes. Open your eyes and share a bit about the experience with one another.

Promote meaningful astral travel experiences with Quartz (Hollandite).

Place a piece of hollandite quartz on your bedside table or slip one inside your pillowcase to promote meaningful astral travel experiences. Place another of these crystals at the base of your bed near your feet to keep your astral body firmly anchored to your physical form. Bring your attention to your physical body and feel yourself connected to both stones. Set an intention for your cosmic journey and gently drift off to sleep while holding this intention in your mind.

Use Astrophyllite to connect with your authentic self.

Make yourself comfortable in a place where you will not be disturbed; your sacred space or a place in nature make excellent locations for this practice. Take your stone in your hands and close your eyes. Visualize yourself becoming grounded and firmly rooted into the Earth. See your light body begin to separate from your physical form, gently rising to the space above your head. Journey with your light body while keeping your physical form grounded. Take your light body through the Earth's atmosphere, out into space, past the stars, past the galaxies, until you reach the very center of the universe. Feel your ego self dissolve away from your being and get in touch with the true essence of your being. When you feel ready, take this true essence of self back down to Earth and feel it merge once again with your physical body, reaffirming your true, authentic self.

Use Staurolite for luck and protection.

Place a staurolite crystal on your altar or in the center of a labyrinth or medicine wheel to amplify its protective and luck-bearing qualities.

WEARING STONES FOR STRENGTH

Wear Amber to relieve grief or shame.

To overcome grief or shame, wear an amber pendant on a long chain so that it hangs over the solar plexus chakra.

Use Tourmaline (Blue) for guidance on your spiritual awakening.

To invite the energy of the Blue Tara goddess into your crystal to help you on your path to spiritual awakening, place your crystal on the eye of a peacock feather. Ask the goddess for wisdom and insight about what needs to be fully realized on your spiritual journey. Sit in quiet meditation and await a response in the stillness.

GETTING PROTECTION FROM SPIRITS

Request protection from nature spirits with Jasper (Kambaba).
Take a piece of kambaba jasper out into nature. Find a place where you feel comfortable and happy, perhaps beneath a tree, in a wildflower meadow, or on the beach. Hold the stone in your hands and request that any nearby nature spirits gather around you. Speak your request for protection to these fairies and other beings and ask that they work with the energy of the stone to support you, keeping you safe and secure. It's best to make your request for protection as specific to your situation as possible, but requesting general protection from the universe is also beneficial. Thank the nature spirits for hearing and responding to your request.

Receive protection from deceased loved ones with Obsidian (Gold Sheen).
Place a piece of gold sheen obsidian on your altar or in your sacred space along with photos of any family members who have crossed over to the other side. Invite your ancestors into your space, letting them know that they are welcome and ask them to keep you safe from harm. Offer to share the stone's energy with them as a way to thank them for their protection and kindness.

Wear Topaz (Imperial Golden) for energy.
Wearing an imperial golden topaz pendant on a long chain over your solar plexus chakra is very beneficial for keeping you energized, but wearing the stone set in a pair of earrings can help you maintain a sunny disposition.

RESOURCES

Websites

AJS Gems
www.ajsgems.com

Amber Lady
Fossil Insects and Amber Jewelry
www.amberlady.com

Ancient Origins
www.ancient-origins.net

Aruarian
www.aruarian.com

Bernadine Fine Art Jewelry
www.bernardine.com

Blue Heron Crystals & Minerals
www.blueheroncrystals.com

Chilean Lapis Lazuli
www.lazulita.cl

Crystal Cure
Gemstone and Crystal Healing
www.crystal-cure.com

Crystal Meanings
www.meanings.crystalsandjewelry.com

Crystal Vaults
www.crystalvaults.com

Dragonfly Amber Jewelry
www.dragonflyamber.com

Fire Mountain Gems and Beads
www.firemountaingems.com

Gem Foundation
Sacred Pipestone Carvings &
Grey Eagle Museum
www.gemfoundation.com

Gem Select
Precious and Semi-Precious
Natural Gemstones
www.gemselect.com

Gemological Institute of America
www.gia.edu

Gemstone Advisor
www.gemstoneadvisor.com

Geology and Earth Science News
www.geology.com

Healing Pendants
Crystal Healing with Meteorites
www.healingpendants.com

Heaven Can Wait
www.heavencanwaitcardsandgifts.
blogspot.com

International Gem Society (IGS)
www.gemsociety.org

Jewels for Me Birthstone Jewelry
www.jewelsforme.com

Lapis Lazuli House
www.lapishouse.com

Mexico Obsidienne
www.mexico-obsidienne.com